THE
HISTORY
BOYS

THE
HISTORY
BOYS

Thirty Iconic Goals
in the History of Nottingham Forest

DAVID MARPLES

First published by Pitch Publishing, 2018

Pitch Publishing
A2 Yeoman Gate
Yeoman Way
Worthing
Sussex
BN13 3QZ
www.pitchpublishing.co.uk
info@pitchpublishing.co.uk

© 2018, Words: David Marples
Art: Sean Hockett

A CIP catalogue record is available for this book
from the British Library.

ISBN 978 1 80150 546 8

Typesetting and origination by Pitch Publishing

Contents

Thank you to Mum and Dad for giving me this football affliction.

Thank you to Jenny and Anya for tolerating this football affliction.

Acknowledgements

Nick M: you are my *centrocampista difensivo*; I owe you more than a few pints. Paul M: all of this started on a rainy Sunday afternoon in The Hop Pole. You were awesome. Jonny O: you've opened so many doors – thank you for your encouragement and support. B&S crew: not sure this book would have happened without this thing we've got going. Sean: thanks for bringing these goals to life with your excellent doodlings. Matt App: your knowledge knows no bounds. Thank you for your patience and pointers. Daniel T: deeply honoured that you took the time to write the foreword; your work is an inspiration.

To anyone who has read any of the numerous ramblings I've churned out down the years, it means a lot. Thank you.

Foreword

WHEN I first heard that David Marples was writing a book about 30 of the most exhilarating moments from supporting this great club I must confess there was a flicker of regret that I had not come up with the idea first.

I know from experience that it is a labour of love to write about Nottingham Forest and, in particular, if it means a nostalgic trip down memory lane to pick out some of the moments when you can actually feel a little sorry for those non-football people who don't 'get it' – on the basis they will never know how much fun they are missing out on.

Living in Manchester now, it's not easy bringing up my son James as a Forest supporter – 'brainwashing', I think the term is – but when I look down the author's choices it is remarkable to think of the places this club has been and how, as a great man once put it, I do hope nobody is stupid enough to write us off.

Sometimes we, as Forest fans, get accused of living too much in the past, and maybe there is a grain of truth in that. Equally, it's 2018 now and the score is still Nottingham 2 London 1 when it comes to European Cups. So why should we overlook the very thing that makes this club famous around the world?

The hardest part for David, I'm sure, was narrowing it down to 30 when, heck, you could probably fill a book of that size just by going through Stan Collymore's portfolio. Stan gets in here because of that howitzer at Peterborough on a day when Forest fans invaded London Road, scaled the floodlights and swarmed over the pitch in the most joyous celebration you could ever imagine. Yet what about the one at Manchester United, the turn and slotted finish at Wolves, the slalom through Sunderland's defence and on and on?

I know how difficult it can be because when I wrote my first book, *Deep Into The Forest*, in 2005 I devoted a chapter each to interviewing 15 of our greatest players – and, as was quickly pointed out, couldn't find the space for Ian Bowyer, Martin O'Neill, Peter Shilton, Frank Clark, Colin Barrett and a good few others.

Sadly, I never got around to writing the sequel – not yet, anyway – but I certainly wouldn't be short of candidates just from the days when we were conquering Europe, being clapped out of Camp Nou and knocking Liverpool off their perch long before Alex Ferguson tried to claim it as his honour.

From my own experience, I can gently warn David therefore to expect a few questions about the omission, for example, of that moment when Johnny Metgod almost decapitated poor old Phil Parkes in the West Ham net, a 35-yard cannonball finished majestically by our funky Dutchman patenting his own pointing-to-the-skies goal celebration, on repeat.

I may even give David a friendly prod to demand that any sequel includes the Garry Parker special against Bristol City that took us to the League Cup Final in the kind of weather conditions at Ashton Gate that Thor himself might have invoked.

Or how about Des Walker versus Luton, Tommy Gaynor at Huddersfield, Lars Bohinen at White Hart Lane and, though he was never really a favourite, Marlon King's last-minute winner against West Ham on the day the City Ground tried to take in the news that Brian Clough had decided it was time, as the banner said, for Heaven XI to get a new manager?

The options are endless but David has done a splendid job of narrowing it down to a list that spans the ages, with 50 years separating Ian Storey-Moore's four-times-and-in FA Cup winner against Everton to Chris Cohen's tension-buster against Ipswich, and I'm particularly pleased Stuart Pearce's late equaliser against Manchester City at Maine Road in the 1992/93 season is also featured.

It probably wasn't our captain's most spectacular goal and it certainly wasn't the happiest season under dear old Cloughie but I was in the away end on the Kippax that day and it was one of those goal celebrations where you can end up 20 yards from where you started. And then, when I had finally come up for oxygen, there was Psycho, held aloft by Nigel Clough, and our skipper had *that* look on his face.

Thank you, Stuart, and all the players who have given us a lifetime of memories and, in particular, the man who walked on the River Trent all those years and got it spot on when he told Don Revie that he wanted to win the league, and do it better.

And thank you, David Marples, for recapturing it all so brilliantly.

Daniel Taylor

Epigraph

'It only takes a second to score a goal.'
Brian Clough

'Sometimes in football, you have to score goals.'
Thierry Henry

'Because it's always got to be blood. Blood is life. Why do you think we eat it? It's what keeps you going, makes you warm, makes you other than dead. Of course it's her blood.'
Spike (Buffy the Vampire Slayer)

'Some people give themselves to religion
Some people give themselves to a cause
Some people give themselves to a lover
I have to give myself to goals.'

Lyrics from 'Straight in at 101' – Los Campesinos!

Introduction

'GOALS change games'. It is a mantra heard many times, most frequently by a manager after their team has conceded – in their eyes at least – a dubious goal, precipitating a humiliating or heavy defeat. Indeed, the existence of an actual 'dubious goals committee' invites more questions than answers.

Goals – dubious or otherwise – are the lifeblood of the football fan. They are the reason you click through the turnstile or travel hundreds of miles on a cold Tuesday evening when the rational part of your head urges you to spend your time doing something more productive or rewarding. It is the carrot of a last-minute winner scored at your end – in front of your fans – that fuels the desire to watch your team. We may occasionally take satisfaction in possession statistics or solid performances or promising debuts but such things are mere fripperies when compared to goals.

They come in all shapes and sizes; some trickle over the line in slow motion while others crash in off the crossbar in glorious explosions. Some are entirely unexpected while others are inevitable. Some are a direct result of individual brilliance while others are the culmination of a fine team move. Regardless of their form, they matter – even the goals against. While those scored by your team provide pure and unadulterated joy, those conceded cause visceral pain and anguish.

Despite the universal circus permanently pitched around the sidelines of football, goals remain the headline act. When football fans come together to share in and celebrate their club's history, it is goals and the players that scored them that are the cornerstone of any discussion. Like the assassination of John Lennon or JFK or the death of Princess Diana or David Bowie, fans recall precisely where they were when certain goals were scored. They are touchstones in the collective history of a club and to individuals, landmarks in the journey of life – providing ballast alongside the pub in which you first got drunk or the school that you attended.

It is with all this in mind that this book unabashedly celebrates pivotal goals – and one save – and the players who scored (or saved) them. Such moments don't exist in a vacuum; context is all. As a result, each piece delves into the career of the player in an attempt to understand the significance of the moment to the club, the player and the fans.

Of course, your favourite goal may well not be included here. Rest assured, it's not because it was deliberately neglected or forgotten. With such a rich and glorious history – especially between 1975 and 1992 – Nottingham Forest provides fertile ground for iconic moments that will live on for, hopefully, another 150 years at least. The original list included at least 50 goals so if your favourite isn't included here, it was almost definitely in the long list.

Where possible, I spoke to individuals in an effort to find out precisely what it feels like to be the one creating history rather than sitting on the sidelines witnessing history unfurl. Sometimes, such people are fully aware of the seismic nature of their achievements while others feel baffled as to the significance of the moment. Either way, if when reading about such goals, you are transported back to that moment in time and space when it occurred – even if it is for a split second – then this book will have achieved its aim.

Speaking to, researching and writing about the subjects of each piece was truly a labour of love. Disappearing down a Nottingham Forest-shaped wormhole for long periods took me back to the terraces, the plastic seats, the incessant rain, the smell of beer and pies and in some cases, being a small boy surrounded by a unified explosion and outpouring of ecstasy.

Goals don't just change games; they change lives.

Ian Storey-Moore
vs Everton (1967)

IN an otherwise unremarkable Portakabin that doubles up as the bar, function room and trophy cabinet for Carlton Town FC on a balmy June evening, history pervades the place like an energy field, surrounding those present and binding them together.

A huge slab of important history stands in the room addressing those present with tales of encounters with George Best and Brian Clough. The man speaking is also a significant part of Nottingham Forest's history himself – woven into the fabric of the club and its supporters for evermore.

The man speaking scored a famous hat-trick for Nottingham Forest in an epic FA Cup quarter-final against Everton in April 1967 – a game akin to Bob Dylan's 'Judas' gig at the Manchester Free Trade Hall a year earlier or to one of the last gigs The Sex Pistols played at Ivanhoe's nightclub in Huddersfield on Christmas Day in 1977.

Seismic events in history are measured not by the amount of people who were actually there to witness them first hand, but by the amount of people who claim they were there.

Ian Storey-Moore is the man speaking.

One man among the small audience listens intently, hooked on Storey-Moore's every word. He applauds loudly – louder than anyone else – when the speaker picks up the microphone. He even hails the speaker as the greatest footballer he has ever seen play. He is a fanboy of the highest order: although a grown man he is currently a wide-eyed child meeting the idol who adorned his bedroom wall. This fanboy isn't like the rest though: there's something different about him. This man too is a monolithic embodiment of football history.

This man is John Robertson.

Robertson declares him to be one of the finest players he's ever seen. Storey-Moore could play a bit.

Storey-Moore signed for Nottingham Forest from Scunthorpe United and went on to make 236 appearances over 11 years, scoring 118 goals. He played as an inside-forward and for many fans competes strongly with Robertson for the title of greatest ever Forest player.

Despite his prolific scoring record he was part of a side that finished just the wrong side of glory, but a team nonetheless that has a special place in the hearts of fans who watched it and deserves to be remembered among the best in the club's history.

As a 17-year-old looking to make a career in the game in 1961, however, life was far from glamorous in those days. Life as a young footballer involved a rotation of jobs including working with the ground staff, cleaning the ground, painting, cleaning boots and that was all in the morning. Once all manner of domestic chores were completed to a satisfactory standard, the afternoons were for training.

But there were no guarantees for the young Storey-Moore that he would make it as a footballer. 'I remember because of the uncertainty my father wanted me to stay on at school,' he told Nottingham Forest periodical *Bandy and Shinty*. 'But myself and David Pleat went to night school and did a journalistic course so we'd keep something in the background in case we didn't make it.'

A wise plan but ultimately, it was his skills with a football rather than a typewriter that would shoot him to prominence.

Arriving as a young player into a Forest squad that had been breaking up after the success of winning the FA Cup in 1959, it took a little time for Storey-Moore to break into the first team. There were established names ahead of him in the wide positions and he had to work hard and bide his time.

Gradually though, Storey-Moore made a name for himself, making more appearances each season until he was a regular choice for the 1966/67 season that would be the pinnacle of the club's achievements in that decade.

As the season began though there wasn't any great sense of anticipation as the man himself remembers it – no feeling that this was going to be a good year. 'No, it was totally unexpected really,' he recounts. 'I think it was the first season we moved to 4-4-2. A new trainer came in called Terry Cavanagh and to be fair to him he was a hard taskmaster, bloody hell you know he really trained hard, so maybe it was him who said we were going to play 4-4-2.'

Such a formation suited this team down to the ground. On his arrival from Birmingham City, Terry Hennessey was shifted from midfield to the back four alongside Bob McKinlay, thus reinventing the big Welshman's talents and allowing him to showcase composure on the ball rather than hurrying and scurrying around in midfield. With Joe Baker and Frank Wignall haring around up front, anything was possible.

The team clicked from the start and things snowballed beautifully from there. Storey-Moore recalled, 'I think it was such a surprise really the way that we started, we didn't really give it a thought to be honest. Then I think it came to maybe February and we thought "blimey, we're still up there". We went to play Man United and I think if we'd won that game we'd have had a real chance. It was a great game; I always remember it because Matt Busby came down, which is very unusual for him.'

Sadly for Forest, Denis Law won the game with an overhead kick but an FA Cup quarter-final against Everton at the City Ground lay in wait. Baker suffered an injury that would keep him out for the rest of the season after a bad challenge by Everton's Brian Labone, but Storey-Moore is forever associated with the tie after scoring a match-winning hat-trick.

It was a truly pulsating affair.

Everton took the lead thanks to a smart strike from number nine Jimmy Husband yet in the second half, their goalkeeper

Andy Rankin spilled a drive from Wignall and Storey-Moore pounced to level. The Trent End heaved and swayed in unison. When Storey-Moore unleashed a left-foot rasper into the corner of the net, putting Forest in the lead, it was a sea of limbs.

The Toffeemen calmed things down by conjuring a rather beautiful equaliser, converted by that man Husband after Sandy Brown bamboozled a Forest defender on the edge of the area.

Not to be outdone, Forest came roaring back and lay siege to the Trent End goal. The Everton defence was creaking and only just survived when a ball was cleared off the line.

⚽ ⚽ ⚽

Time is ticking. Lump it forward. Get it in the mixer.

Wignall does exactly that. Storey-Moore latches on to a knockdown, gets in front of his man and scuffs a shot, which Rankin can only parry back into play. Storey-Moore duly nods it goalbound, ensuring he gets the requisite height to keep it out of the reach of Rankin, laying helpless like an upturned beetle on the floor. The ball hits the bar and bounces down on the goal line.

Since his initial shot, Storey-Moore has been in perpetual motion – a whizz of arms and legs. It's third time lucky as he nods in from close range, inciting absolute and unadulterated bedlam in the Trent End.

⚽ ⚽ ⚽

Typically though, Storey-Moore today holds up his team-mate Wignall as the star performer, even though the fans often turn to that game as a highlight of his time at the club. He says, 'I didn't think I played particularly well. In the first half we never got going at all to be honest with you. Everton were the better team and then suddenly it took off in the second half.

'I think the star player was Frank Wignall that day. He was a real handful. I think he made all three goals for me if I remember right. An ex-Evertonian he was and I think it was down to him how we won it. For a lot of my goals, balls seemed to come into the box and Frank got something on it and it seemed to drop to me. He could look after himself – we got quite close, Frank and I.'

With Baker sidelined the team struggled to maintain their momentum. Manchester United became champions and would go on to win the European Cup the following season, while in the FA Cup Jimmy Greaves and Frank Saul broke Forest's hearts, scoring for Tottenham Hotspur in a 2-1 victory at Hillsborough before going on to beat Chelsea in the final. It had been a case of so close and yet so far but the club was unable, or unwilling, to build on that impressive season.

Although the FA Cup game is perhaps the one most associated with Storey-Moore, his greatest ever goal for Forest was surely against Arsenal in 1971. The game finished 1-1 but Bob Wilson described the goal as the best ever scored against him after Storey-Moore had picked up the ball from his own goalkeeper before running the length of the pitch to slot home.

'At Arsenal, yes, on Boxing Day,' he ponders. 'It was Alan Ball's debut for Arsenal and all I can remember to this day is that I could just see his white boots trailing behind me and I just kept going and going and then I was suddenly confronted by this wall of yellow at the edge of the box. I thought I've got this far and suddenly, I don't how I did it, I was just faced with Bob Wilson five yards out and the first thought that comes to you then is for God's sake don't miss it now.'

When he did finally decide to leave the transfer itself became another notable story in his career. With two clubs vying for his signature and Forest keen to make sure that he didn't follow the likes of Hennessey and Alan Hinton to their major rivals, negotiations became a farce and Storey-Moore was stuck between Matt Gillies and some young buck – then manager of Derby County – by the name of Brian Clough.

This simply complicated matters. Storey-Moore was called in one Friday morning and told by Gillies that two clubs had agreed a fee. He knew this full well since Manchester United and Derby had both been in touch with him already. Gillies told him that he should speak to United first so he met manager Frank O'Farrell, Gillies, assistant manager Bill Anderson and club secretary Ken Smales. Agreeing personal terms proved difficult though and negotiations broke down.

Gillies agreed to get Clough on the phone and from then, things moved fast. Clough and Peter Taylor raced to meet Storey-Moore within 30 minutes. 'So I'm sat there in trepidation, you can imagine with those two, you didn't like to say no did you? They came in the room and to be fair to them they were a good side then, had some good players, so I signed for them,' he recalls.

Clough elected to go to the City Ground in an effort to, in his words, 'sort that lot out'. While he did so, Storey-Moore dined with the Derby players that evening as they prepared for a fixture against Wolves the following day. At that stage, all concerned were operating under the impression that Storey-Moore was a Derby County player, even though nothing had been signed yet. Nonetheless, Clough was confident he had his man.

Storey-Moore looks back, 'Then I was on the pitch; I was really embarrassed afterwards. Anyway, Busby and O'Farrell came to the house on the Monday and I signed for them. The [Forest] chairman had said there's no way you're going to Derby County.'

Storey-Moore maintains that the whole embarrassing affair wasn't his fault and although him signing for United didn't go down well with Clough, bridges were eventually repaired. He says, 'I saw him when Paul Hart was the manager and I was working with Paul. I think he was speaking at a dinner and he walks in and he suddenly turns round and sees me and says, "Oh, it's you is it? They tell me you're not as big a shithouse as you used to be." But that was him.'

Storey-Moore was unfortunate not to add to his one international cap, which came against Holland in 1970. Although injury later curtailed his career in England, the final curtain didn't quite come down as after a couple of years' rest there was enough of a recovery for him to try something completely new and head out to the USA to play in the North American Soccer League. Having sampled life abroad, a new opportunity emerged back at home to try his hand at management at Burton Albion, followed by a period of scouting back at Forest.

Those present at the City Ground in 1967 to witness Storey-Moore's historical hat-trick witnessed history unfolding in front of them – events that would be discussed and written about 50 years later.

He recalls, 'When we played, when you scored a goal or you had a good game, you never even thought about money. It was that elation and the buzz you got from the crowd, scoring a winning goal, or being on a winning side. There was the song "Give it to Moore, he will score" and you'd think, well, I've got to now, haven't I?

'If you had that empathy with the fans you wanted to do well for them. In those days it was a bit more of a cloth cap image, they'd come from the factory and it was a relief to come and see your team. If you could make them happy you would.'

Peter Shilton vs Coventry City (1978)

PETER Shilton never has a cold head. Granted, being blessed with hair as thick, tight and curly as springs for a dollhouse bed is part of the reason why his cranium need never experience a chill. But beyond that, should the cold ever permeate his seemingly hermetically-sealed skull, he could always reach for one of his 125 England caps to warm himself up.

Making his debut in 1970 and rather symmetrically, his final appearance for England 20 years later, Shilton was a colossus between the sticks for a full two decades. Amazingly, Shilton might well have acquired even more caps were England manager Ron Greenwood a little less fair-minded since for a period, net-guarding duties for the national team rotated between Shilton and Ray Clemence, who himself acquired 61 caps.

Imagine that – Shilton could quite feasibly be the owner of 186 caps, a figure that would see him top the charts for international appearances, a position currently held by Ahmed Hassan with 184 for Egypt.

That's more caps than a black and white photograph of a football crowd in Barnsley in the 1950s.

With such a glittering and elongated England career, it is easy to disassociate Shilton with domestic football, especially given that he racked up more than 175 appearances each for no fewer than four clubs.

His five-year stint working under Brian Clough between 1977 and 1982 meant that not only were Forest the team for whom he made his second most appearances (hometown and first club Leicester City being the most) but this period just happened to coincide with the time when Nottingham Forest were hoovering up silverware like a Dyson let loose on a student floor. Coincidence? Absolutely not.

Clough was obsessed with keeping the opposition out of his goal and although his team's start to the title-winning season of 1977/78 was a blistering one, he looked to shore up his defence as quickly and effectively as he could.

While Forest opened with an impressive mauling of a very decent Everton side that would ultimately finish third, Shilton was enduring a horrible game at Mansfield Town's Field Mill where his newly-relegated Stoke City team were served with their arses on a plate in a 2-1 defeat.

Forest were steamrollering all comers, winning their opening three games and conceding only one goal. Then September came around and a first defeat, at Arsenal, was followed by a win against Wolves.

However, Clough was concerned at the concession of five goals in these two games. He wanted the best and knew where to find him.

'I knew Brian,' Shilton recollects. 'He tried to sign me when he was at Derby. He tried to sign me when he was at Leeds. I'd met him before I came to Forest and I knew him reasonably well but obviously to play under him and have him manage me was terrific. From the minute he started it was just a dream come true. I didn't really get too much stick from him.

'I saw the side that got promotion by the skin of their teeth and thought that they weren't bad; they could play and score goals. But obviously I never thought that it would be so fast. I knew Brian Clough was a man that wanted success and somebody that I respected a lot in football and somebody I wanted to play under. It was just a dream come true. It happened so quickly – we won the league, won two European Cups...I don't think anybody could say they *expected* that but it was certainly fantastic to be part of it.'

Besides, who among us wouldn't stand in a field in Mansfield not wishing to be elsewhere?

Clough's assistant, Peter Taylor, knew a thing or two about goalkeeping and like his mate knew exactly what Shilton would bring to the table. In his book, *With Clough by Taylor,* he expressed his admiration for the England man, 'Signing Peter was a highlight of my career, for I had been obsessed with him since he was 19 and already a fixture in Leicester City's first team. I travelled regularly from Derby to watch Shilton when he replaced the celebrated Gordon Banks.

'The boy's maturity and technique were astonishing; he knew instinctively the tricks of a trade that normally demands a long apprenticeship. I admired his bravery, his handling and his temperament, but was impressed most of all by this teenager's mastery of positional play and marshalling defences – the arts that most keepers learn late.'

He made his debut in September, wearing his trademark green jersey and chalking up a clean sheet in a 2-0 win against Aston Villa. This was the first of a mind-boggling 23 shut-outs in 37 appearances in the league that season. No wonder Brian loved him and that green top so much.

Clough knew from the start who the better keeper was between Shilton and Clemence – he had no time for daintily stepping around the issue like Greenwood did. In *Walking on Water*, Clough wrote, 'I keep going back to Ron Greenwood and the problem he had in deciding between the merits of Peter Shilton and Ray Clemence – and he was the man who landed the job I went for! No disrespect to Clemence whatsoever but, in my judgement, Shilton was just that little better.'

Shilton himself is keen to deflect credit to the team: 'Good players. Good players who got on with the job and played as a team. They were all good individuals. All strong characters in their own way but honest – we all played for each other and a great management team. If he [Brian] was here, we wouldn't be talking like this – he'd be doing the talking. We'd be sitting in the background doing a job.'

The league title was secured at Highfield Road in a 0-0 draw. It should not be forgotten that this was a team that had only won promotion to the top league less than a year ago, and a mere two years previously were languishing in the lower reaches of the Second Division. 'To win the league at Coventry, we got a 0-0 when we only needed a point and I had a pretty good game that day – I made a save that people remember. So to win the league in your first season, having got promotion was fantastic,' Shilton says.

To call it 'a save that people remember' is as far from over-egging the pudding as can be – it's erecting a ten-foot high wall between the pudding and a batch of eggs.

'It was on the near post,' Shilton recalls. 'Ian Wallace was in the box to the byline and he chipped it, just inside the six-yard box. I just got across the goal and it was an instinctive save. It's one of those that all the work on the training pitch, all the hard work on reactions and agility just came off. It's not very often you remember the saves when you're a goalkeeper but it does get replayed a few times. It was an iconic day because we won the league and that made it even sweeter.'

⚽ ⚽ ⚽

It is a remarkable save. He flings his huge paws up in the air to claw the ball over the bar. Mick Ferguson, whose bullet header Shilton has kept out, is having trouble comprehending what just happened. He's all set to raise his arms aloft and start charging around like a man who has just put a dent in the bumper of the champions elect and secured a very respectable seventh place in the table. Not now though. Not now the bear in green has denied him. Ferguson sinks to his knees. He's not angry. He's not disappointed. He just doesn't understand.

Shilton is back on his feet and busy doing what any self-respecting goalkeeper should do having just rescued their team – pointing the finger at whoever allowed the opposition to get so close to scoring and telling them exactly what they should have done to prevent it.

It's vintage Shilton: spring to your feet and forcefully explain to the defenders that if they did their jobs, he wouldn't have to leap around like a loon and risk muddy knees or green stains to his pristine jersey. If all of this could be accompanied by a sustained bout of finger-wagging indicating precisely where the defenders failed to carry out the most basic of tasks then all the better. It's an endearing trait he exercised throughout his career.

⚽ ⚽ ⚽

More trophies would come during his time at Forest, with the second European Cup win a particularly pleasing moment. Asked what his proudest occasion was in a Forest jersey, Shilton concludes, 'I think winning the European Cup the second time against Hamburger SV. We were really under-strength and we'd had about 75 games [64 competitive games] that year. We were shattered. Keegan and Hamburg were the favourites but we managed to do a "backs to the wall" job and beat them 1-0 so those two games in particular were pretty memorable.'

Again, Shilton declines to mention his string of world-class saves that kept the Germans out, most notably an athletic leap to tip Peter Nogly's long-range effort over the bar.

After this game though, there would be no more club honours for Shilton to claim. Having lifted the First Division title, one League Cup, one Charity Shield, one European Super Cup and a couple of European Cups, Shilton left Forest for Southampton in 1982 to join up with, coincidentally, Kevin Keegan, who returned to British shores from his successful stint in Germany. Together, they played a key role in helping the Saints to a second-place finish in 1984, just three points behind Liverpool.

Bizarrely, in his final season at Forest in 1981/82, Shilton was part of a team that finished 12th with 57 points and a record reading W15 D12 L15. In his first season at Southampton the season after, Shilton repeated the very same trick. The Saints finished in 12th position having won 15, drawn 12 and lost 15.

The next time someone suggests that lightning never strikes twice in the same place, refer him or her to this statistic.

Five years at Southampton followed with another standard five years at Derby County, until his appearances grew more sporadic, and then came an unsuccessful tenure as manager at Plymouth Argyle. In December 1996, Shilton made his 1,000th career club appearance, for Leyton Orient in a 2-0 win against Brighton. He didn't expect 'all this palaver really'. It seems that to him, waking up and standing between the sticks while leaping around preventing the ball going between the aforementioned sticks is simply what one does with one's time.

Shilton leapt around between the sticks for 30 years and what's more, he did it exceptionally well. It might be said that he was lucky to have played for Nottingham Forest while they lifted pretty much every major honour available but it might be more truthful to say that Forest were lucky to have him to help them do so.

Frank Clark vs
Ipswich Town (1978)

REPETITION is overrated. As long as you do something well, there's a case to be made that you only need to do it the once. Einstein only developed the theory of relativity once, Bowie only wrote and recorded 'Heroes' once and Frank Clark only scored the one goal. Sometimes, once is enough.

Clark's place in the fabric of Nottingham Forest cannot be underestimated. Player, manager, chairman and club ambassador; he hasn't just *got* the t-shirt, he designed, printed and flogged the t-shirt in a megastore while developing an internet start-up company manufacturing and promoting t-shirts which he later sold for billions of pounds. In many ways, Frank Clark *is* Nottingham Forest.

After 389 appearances for Newcastle United and at the age of 32, Clark was released and Brian Clough couldn't believe his luck on signing him in 1975. Clough loved Frank. Everybody, it seems, loved Frank. In his autobiography, Clough went all gooey and saccharine sweet when it came to Frank, 'I can still see Frank Clark sitting at the back of the team coach strumming away, singing in a lovely soft voice with his team-mates gathered round and joining in. Country or middle-of-the-road or whatever they called it, I was never quite sure. [Peter] Taylor used to spin round in his seat and shout, "Not another one of those bloody songs, Frank!" He didn't mean it. Taylor appreciated Frank's songs as much as any of us. He knew the importance of "togetherness" in a team. Clark and his guitar entertained us not only throughout the country but across Europe.'

Clough's long-term coach, Alan Hill, recalls the moment Brian learned of his successor as manager. It was a messy period and Clough was one of the last to know that Clark would take up the reins from him in 1993. Hill wasn't keen to break the news but on the other hand, certainly wasn't going to conceal the truth from his boss. An end-of-season trip to Spain was planned but Hill couldn't go. Initially, as Hill explained to Nottingham Forest periodical *Bandy and Shinty*, Clough couldn't comprehend the situation:

'What do you mean?'

'I can't – the chairman says I'm to stay here, and look after the new manager.'

'The new what?'

'The new manager.'

And you can see, it rocks him. 'You mean to tell me that you know they've appointed a new manager, and I don't?'

'I think so.'

'Who is it?'

'Frank.'

'Frank who?'

'*Frank.*'

'*Our* Frank?' And he thinks about it, and there's a bit of warmth. He liked Frank, a lot. 'Well you stop here, then. And make sure you look after him.'

Clough knew that Our Frank would need all the support he could get as he set out to take on the rather enviable task of replacing him as manager, made all the more difficult given that Forest were now in the second tier of English football. Talk about big shoes to fill – Our Frank was like a toddler who's just discovered their dad's slippers and is waddling around in the ridiculously oversized footwear to great comedic and endearing effect.

Except, this wasn't a farce. Clark had spent eight years serving his apprenticeship in management at Leyton Orient in very demanding circumstances. He told *When Saturday Comes*, 'Orient was the hardest job simply because of lack of money until the last few years when Tony Wood, who'd made a fortune in the coffee business, took over. I mention in the book that I was once told to raise 15 grand in four weeks to stop the club going out of business. It seems like a small amount today but it put us under huge pressure at the time.'

Under Clark's management, the O's moved from the bottom tier to the third, only narrowly missing out on a play-off place in the 1992/93 season. He was ready and he was anointed.

Not content with playing a key role in dragging Forest up from the obscurity of the second tier to becoming domestic and European champions as a player, he came pretty close to repeating the feat as a manager. Promotion back to the Premier League was secured at the first time of asking and Forest's third-place finish as a newly-promoted club to the top tier remains a record placing for debutants in the Premier League. On the back of this magnificent achievement, European football returned to Trentside for the first time since the infamous defeat to RSC Anderlecht in 1984.

Throughout this sojourn into Europe though, Our Frank remained the Frank Clark he always was. Young starlet Paul McGregor found an unlikely kinship with his boss and bonded over music, 'I remember standing at the airport going out to AJ Auxerre surrounded by press and he put his bag down and there was Danny Sugarman's book on The Doors, *No One Here Gets Out Alive* sticking out of his bag. "Gaffer, I love The Doors." So we had a chat about them for ten minutes.'

When Clough wrote in *Walking on Water* that 'we loved him – everybody loved Frank Clark – but management, certainly team management, just wasn't in him as far as I could see. He is far better suited to the administrative side of the business', he was perhaps selling his reliable left-back a little short. There can be no doubt that those who came into Clark's orbit loved him. Brian loved him.

Even those players who Clark didn't fancy seemed to love him. In *Looking After No.1,* Mark Crossley wears an 'I heart Frank' badge. 'I love Frank Clark. I have the utmost respect for him, as a manager and a man. I had a feeling he didn't rate me,' he writes.

But it's not just love for the man that so many had and still have: it's respect too. When Clark spoke, his team-mates – who held him in such high regard – listened.

In Daniel Taylor's *I Believe In Miracles*, the fruits of Clark's foresight can be found as Clark spotted young striker Garry Birtles feeling sorry for himself on the coach back from an away game.

He says, 'His chin was on the floor. I just tried to offer him a bit of support, because I could see he was very down. He said he felt like his career wasn't going anywhere, that Clough clearly didn't rate him very much and he was going to pack up and go back to being a carpet-layer.'

Then came some sage advice, 'If it's only a year, sit tight. You never know what's round the corner in football.'

Birtles would go on to break into the first team in spectacular style, scoring in the first round of the European Cup against Liverpool. Who knows what might have happened were Birtles to have ignored Clark's wise words?

But before he would steer the good ship Nottingham Forest into calmer waters as manager and later chairman, there was the small matter of matching Peter Shilton's scoring tally. One would be enough.

With the First Division title secured three days previously at Coventry City, a League Cup in the bag and European football to look forward to, the pressure was off for a midweek visit to Portman Road.

Our Frank takes up the story, 'So that's the scenario – we'd won the league on the Saturday, Ipswich were playing in the FA Cup Final two weeks later. It was a midweek game and I was sub – there was only one sub.

'So you can imagine it wasn't much of a game. The first half was quite poor really – 0-0. Then came half-time and obviously BC wasn't very happy. And Withey being Withey – Peter Withe – could never keep his mouth shut and chipped back at him. So

Cloughie said, "You. Off. Get in the bath." He pointed at me and said, "Get warmed up."

'So I'm warming up and I'm looking around and thinking – I think Ian Bowyer was playing left-back – he'll probably move him up top and I'll play left-back. The bell goes and he still hasn't said anything. I said, "Boss, where do you want me to play?" "Go and play up front – you can't be any worse than him."

'So I go and play up front and all the lads are laughing at me. Ipswich had a big centre-back called Allan Hunter. I knew him quite well because he was a cousin of Willie McFaul who was goalkeeper when I played at Newcastle. So first chance I get, I run in close to him – "I know you want to play in that cup final next week so if you don't fucking kick me, I won't kick you." We had a laugh about it.'

You can safely file Allan Hunter in the drawer labelled 'uncompromising 1970s defender', as this nugget from Terry Butcher's autobiography testifies in which he describes an incident where Butcher 'crossed himself' during a reserve match. 'Big Allan Hunter was sitting in the stand and after the game he grabbed me and asked me if I was a Catholic. I told him I wasn't. I was an English Protestant. Why, then, he asked, did I cross myself? I told him it was for luck but he told me to remember I was a Protestant and warned me never to do it again – if I did, he would really sort me out.'

Clearly Hunter was not a man to be messed with – and certainly not someone to start kicking. Our Frank – wise as ever – was using his nous and making people generally like him.

'Anyway, the game carried on and it wasn't getting any better,' Clark continues. 'We got a corner – first corner in 70 minutes. I'm in the penalty area and I'm a bit embarrassed, I don't know where to go: I've never been there. Of course, with Brian there were no set piece routines, you just went where it took you. So I thought I'd hover around the six-yard box.

'So Robbo [John Robertson] chips this corner in and somehow it dropped right on my foot, four yards out – even I couldn't miss. Right foot too.

'The place erupted. All the lads went berserk. Cloughie and [Peter] Taylor were off the bench and of course, the Ipswich crowd couldn't understand what was going on. Anyway, we finished up winning the game 2-0. Brian said it was one of his greatest achievements!

'At the end of the game, Peter Taylor went to see Bobby Robson to see if he could get the match ball. Bobby couldn't believe it – "You're trying to tell me that he's played 500 league games and that's his first goal?!"

'I actually got the ball though. Everybody signed it too.'

Imagine being Peter Withe at this point. Joint top scorer for the season with 19 goals and Frank bloody-no-goals-bloody-Clark has just bagged one within 33 minutes of taking your place.

What's more, everyone seems to really really love Frank Clark.

Withe probably didn't take it well. 'Not happy,' says Clark. 'It might have precipitated his move but there was also a contract issue.'

Clough too recalled the seismic event with similarly nostalgic reverence in his autobiography, 'That was the day I pulled off Peter Withe and sent on Frank as substitute. He turned to me on the touchline, and asked, with that endearing little lisp of his, "Where do you want me to play, boss?"

'"Bloody well play at centre-forward," I said. "I've just pulled Withey off, haven't I? The full-backs are doing brilliantly, so get yourself up front."

'So up he went, and scored his first ever league goal at the age of 32. Tony Woodcock, who was sitting next to me in the dugout said, "You do realise the others will never get a bloody ball from Frank again." Sure enough, every time Clark got the ball after that he turned with it and ran for goal, oblivious to team-mates either side of him.

'"Look at him," Woodcock shouted. "Just look at him. One bloody goal in his life and he's after a hat-trick!" We won the match.'

For Frank and Hunter, all's well that ends well. Ipswich went on to defeat Arsenal in the FA Cup Final thanks to a late winner from Roger Osborne, who having bagged the goal promptly went and fainted with the emotion of it all. Hunter got his winner's medal and Our Frank got his goal – his single, solitary goal.

Of course, Our Frank didn't *need* a goal to worm his way into the hearts of the Forest faithful – he'd done that anyway and by returning as manager, chairman, ambassador and all-round latter day Geordie Jimmy Stewart/Tom Hanks figure, truly cemented his place in Forest folklore. Yet a goal is always nice.

Besides, being Frank, he only needed to do it once.

Colin Barrett vs
Liverpool (1978)

DOORS are important: always have been, always will be. Not only do they keep the cold out, but also unwanted strangers too. Once closed, you can do what you like... within reason.

Il Duomo di Firenze (The Cathedral in Florence) is just one of an incalculable number of places to have doors. It's a quite magnificent structure, boasting a clock designed in 1443 by Paolo Uccello, which still accurately calculates the hours of daylight remaining each day. But the real significance here is the doors.

Back in 1401, it was decided that some new ones were required and so the usual course of action was set in motion: put the contract out to tender. But they weren't just any old doors: these were the doors of the Duomo. Rival geniuses Lorenzo Ghiberti and Filippo Brunelleschi locked horns to win the contract to build the required bronze doors.

Ghiberti's fusion of Gothic and Naturalism in terms of style got him the gig and, it is claimed by some, kick-started the Renaissance: the pushing aside of ignorance in favour of curiosity in the scientific, leading to the recognition that it was the sun around which Earth orbited and not the other way round. The realisation that previously unexplained events could actually be accounted for and were not to be feared due to random superstition reduced fear of the world around us. The Renaissance sparked our curiosity to prod, to poke, to question the world around us and in doing so, achieve magnificent things.

It is from such small whims that momentous events are borne. A provincial football team lifting the European Cup merely four years since languishing mid-table in the second tier is one of those – miraculous even.

But if the start of the Renaissance can be (arguably) distilled down to a single event or moment, so can the miracle of the double-European Cup-winning team; specifically to around the 87th minute of the first leg of the first round between upstarts Nottingham Forest and reigning European champions Liverpool. It was in this moment that Colin Barrett strode forward and scored the second goal to give his team an ultimately unassailable lead going into the second leg.

'If you'd have said right from Cloughie's first moment walking into Nottingham Forest Football Club, when they were 13th or 14th in the second tier of football, and turned around to the chairman at the time and said, "Well, I'll get you out of this division, I'll then win the next division [the top tier], I'll then get the club to the European Cup and I'll win it and then I'll retain it the next season and just throw in a couple of League Cups in-between. I'll do all that in four years. Will you give me the job?" I think they'd send him to the loony house.'

These are the words of the scorer of that all-important goal, and Barrett has a point. The rise of the football club under Brian Clough is a miraculous tale and although it's fair to say that at this stage in their development (the team were league champions after all) the shakedown of the reigning European champions and the runners-up to their own championship-winning season was, if not a shock, then certainly a seismic moment in the shift in power among the top branches of English and European football.

⚽ ⚽ ⚽

Like Ghiberti's masterpiece, the goal too is a fusion, combining grace and determination. The assured finish is a thing of beauty but determination is evident in the build-up, which starts on the halfway line as Barrett heroically blocked not once, but twice. But he isn't finished yet – in fact he is just getting started.

He gallops on as Garry Birtles, inspired by his debut goal earlier on in the game, carries the ball forward to his left. As Birtles chips the ball into the area on to the head of Tony Woodcock, Barrett reaches the six-yard line. Inside, he's a bit worried since he knows Cloughie and Taylor will be yelling at him and asking what on earth he thinks he's doing, or some other words to that effect. After all, this is the 87th minute and a one-goal lead is preferable to a 1-1 draw to take to Anfield.

No time for that now though, as Woodcock cushions the ball back to him with his beautifully coiffured head of hair. The next time the ball touches the ground is when it comes off the back of the net, after being rifled first time past Ray Clemence before he's even had time to adjust his feet, never mind react. Woodcock tries to grab Barrett for a celebratory hug, but there's no stopping him. He's gone. He shrugs him off – telling him to politely go away – and runs, runs, runs in utter ecstasy.

Nottingham Forest are on their way to being champions of Europe.

⚽⚽⚽

Barrett himself is keen for the approach work to be acknowledged, and rightly so. 'Nobody ever shows you the goal in its entirety – they only ever show the finish. I block Phil Neal's attempted pass and the ball flies down to Birtles on the left-hand side.' It's the 87th minute and the left-back goes tearing upfield – Jose Mourinho would be experiencing severe convulsions, never mind the fact that Clough is sitting in the dugout. Perhaps fortunately for Barrett though, he's on the other flank, far away and out of earshot of Clough and Taylor.

But Barrett was just doing what came naturally, especially in a team brimming with confidence. Besides, he was also doing what every footballer fortunate to play under Clough was told – keep it simple and do your job to the very best of your ability. It matters not a jot the stage of the game, where it is being played, whether you're a million-pound signing or a green and wet behind the ears apprentice – you play what's in front of you.

He recalls, 'You go and support, you block one, you block two. It's gone to Birtles and he's making a run down the left-hand side and I just thought, "I've got to get up there." He's then gone around [Phil] Thompson and whipped in a fantastic cross. Woody [Tony Woodcock] gets his head on the end of it and he cushions it like a dream and I've just smashed it in the net. It sounds simple really!'

But was it really part of the plan to be gallivanting like a troubadour at such a vital stage in the game? Barrett's wingman on that occasion, and on so many others, was the genius that is John Robertson. As talented and magical as he was, the thought of the 'Picasso of our game' filling in at left-back while Liverpool went in search of an equaliser would not be a reassuring one for Forest supporters.

Barrett remembers the reaction from the dugout, 'As I start to go forward [Clough and Taylor] are saying, "Where is that idiot going? Where's he going now? What is he doing?" They're shouting, "Get back! Get back!" Then all of a sudden, "GOAL!" Martin O Neill [the substitute that evening] told me how he could still remember Peter Taylor later deadpanning, "We encourage our full-backs to go forward."'

To watch the left-back signed from Manchester City three years previously maraud forward is a joy to behold. After doing his job meticulously by winning the ball on the halfway line, he strides forward – always looking around to check his whereabouts and the position of those around him. This is not just tearing forward without a care in the world, on the hunt for personal glory – he is fully aware of everything around him.

But as he approaches the penalty area, his pace slows – perhaps doubt, or even fear, has started to hit him, 'I ended up in the furthest part of the ground away from our goal and if they go and score, I am really in the muck.'

But once the ball came in to Woodcock, there was little danger of a Liverpool breakaway. Before anyone could draw breath and appreciate Woodcock's cushioned header and think to themselves, 'That's a lovely knock-down, maybe he has a chance here,' the ball was in the net after the left-back spun and adjusted his body shape to blast the ball beyond Clemence. Woodcock tried to grab him but Barrett was having none of it. He was off, '"Eff off! I'm on my way!" I've pushed him out of the way and I'm gone!'

Those of a certain age will recall Italy's Marco Tardelli wheeling away in sheer exultation after scoring against West Germany in the 1982 World Cup Final. Such an iconic image conjures up the absolute pleasure of scoring a goal in a high stakes game that us mere mortals cannot comprehend. Barrett's celebrations, like Tardelli's, go some way towards capturing such unadulterated and pure joy. He was in a world of his own before Viv Anderson appeared and leaped into his path to impede his progress. To be fair, Barrett had already slowed down; perhaps the moment was starting to catch up with him.

After that, all of the Forest players wanted a piece of him.

But the tie wasn't over, only the first leg. The cushion that Barrett's goal provided was crucial though and altered the complexion of the second leg. 'It gave the team confidence going into the away leg. We could hold on to a lead of some sort,' said Barrett.

Indeed, Forest only conceded 24 goals in the previous season on their way to the league title. Furthermore, Clough's team was in the midst of a record-breaking 42-game unbeaten run, spanning back ten months to November 1977. By the time Liverpool arrived at the City Ground for this tie in September 1978, Forest had conceded only 16 goals in the whole run – and three of those came in one game, away at Norwich City in February while Clough was on a mid-season holiday in Majorca.

With Peter Shilton between the sticks, the fearsome pairing of Larry Lloyd and Kenneth Burns at centre-back and Barrett and Anderson setting the mould for the modern-day full-backs in their desire to get forward, this was a formidable defensive unit. Just for good measure, John McGovern patrolled the back four with stealth and skill. Of course, the lads fancied their chances of keeping a clean sheet at Anfield – which they duly did, playing out a reasonably comfortable 0-0 draw.

Disposing of Liverpool was a huge hurdle for this Forest team in their first European tie. Initially, the squad were a tad disappointed to draw them after getting all giddy about which far-flung destinations and exotic teams they envisaged pitting their wits against. But once the reigning champions were out of the way, there was little to fear.

The record books state that Forest went on to beat AEK Athens, Grasshopper Club Zurich and FC Köln. Needless to say, all these clubs were reigning champions in their own leagues. Although Grasshopper may not send shivers down the spine of the modern football fan weaned on the Premier League, they saw off a Real Madrid side boasting Uli Stielike, Vicente del Bosque and Juanito – a team that were reigning La Liga champions and would go on to reclaim their title the following year.

In May 1979, McGovern lifted the European Cup in Munich after John Roberston sent over a teasing cross for Trevor Francis to head home. Unthinkably, the team went on to successfully defend their crown and only went and lifted the darn thing again, this time in Madrid after Robertson's goal against a Kevin Keegan and Felix Magath-inspired Hamburg team.

Without the cushion of Barrett's goal in the embryonic stages of Forest's European odyssey, one wonders whether the side might have progressed so far and achieved so much. Of course we'll never know, and their defensive record suggests that they may well have stood firm against the inevitable Liverpool onslaught of the second leg regardless. But cushions are lovely things to possess and snuggle up to: they offer comfort and in turn inspire confidence. Barrett's tenacious blocks and adventurousness arguably shaped the club's history.

In a slightly sad ending, Barrett missed out on the final after sustaining an ultimately career-threatening injury. He did play in the gloriously bonkers semi-final first leg against FC Köln at the City Ground, the 3-3 draw that, courtesy of their away goals, gave the German team the edge. Nevertheless, Ian Bowyer's header in the away tie edged Forest through.

Barrett never fully recovered from his injury and did not feature in the subsequent European Cup Final of 1980 either. He left Forest in that year for Swindon Town but his knee eventually gave way. He has no regrets though, and points out that he did play in the 1979 League Cup Final victory against Southampton.

Neither is he sick of talking about 'that goal'. He says, 'I don't get frustrated with it. I know it's meant a great deal to an awful lot to people. A lot of my fellow players have always mentioned it too. From my point of view, I never get fed up with it. It's always the first thing anybody says to me anyway! Everybody says, "I was there." I've had about 70,000 people say they were there!'

Indeed, few footballers would so happily revel in such an iconic goal. In September 2017, the Nottingham Forest supporter-driven movement Forza Garibaldi laid on some boats for fans to drink beer, sing songs and make merry on the morning of a game against Sheffield United. At one stage, a Subbuteo pitch materialised and Barrett was asked whether he would recreate his goal using those broad-based players, an oversized ball, a pitch desperately in need of some serious ironing and a goalkeeper attached to a long stick.

Barrett went one better. Not for him such fiddly accoutrements: if he was going to recreate the goal, he was going to do it properly. He clambered aboard the pitch and with an oversized shoe, volleyed the ball into the net. Again.

Every great achievement, era or epoch has a starting point or moment in time that can, in retrospect, be recognised as defining ones. It is people like Lorenzo Ghiberti and Colin Barrett who produce such moments that shape history. Without these, the world might look slightly different.

John McGovern vs AEK Athens (1978)

A SHIP without a rudder is pretty useless. The world's most expensive yacht is the *History Supreme* at $4.5bn. This staggering sum is owed to the solid gold and platinum used to assemble this luxury liner, which features no less than 100,000kg (220,000lb) of these precious metals. They adorn the entirety of the boat right from the base of the vessel, coated in a thin layer of solid gold, to the dining area, deck, rails, staircases and anchor. The master bedroom boasts a wall feature made from meteorite rock and a statue made from genuine Tyrannosaurus Rex bones – a statement which simply raises more questions than answers.

Yet even a princely construction like this requires a rudder – something to plonk in the water so as to steer all of the lavish paraphernalia on board in the right direction. If John Robertson was Brian Clough's Picasso, John McGovern was the guy who made and delivered the canvas on to which Picasso wowed the world.

Signed by Clough in 1965 for Hartlepools United, McGovern would follow Clough to Derby County, Leeds United and to Nottingham Forest where he would captain the side to an Anglo-Scottish Cup, a First Division title, two League Cups, an FA Charity Shield, two European Cups and a European Super Cup. Clough selected McGovern to play for him approximately 500 times across four different clubs. When someone like Clough sticks your name on the team sheet so frequently, you clearly have something to offer.

In Tony Francis's *Clough: A Biography*, McGovern recalls meeting the man that would shape so much of his professional career and upbringing, 'The first time I met him I was petrified. He shook my hand and said, "Get you hair cut, stand up straight and push your shoulders back." It was unnerving for a 16-year-old but when the fear subsided, I worshipped everything he did and said. As a young lad without a father, I was only too happy to do as he commanded. He made me feel like a giant on the football field.'

Clough tended to have that effect on people but at the time, no one with a speck of grey matter in their heads could have possibly imagined the glittering career ahead for both men. Young and brash in his first management role at Hartlepools, Clough sought permission from McGovern's school. In his autobiography, Clough wrote, 'As soon as the headmaster gave his permission I was out of there, knowing that I'd made one of the most significant signings of that era. McGovern, who followed me first to Derby County and then to Nottingham Forest, went on to lift more trophies than any A Levels he might have gained had he stayed at school. How many team captains have lifted that mighty European Cup above their head in successive seasons?'

Not many. In fact, just the one as it happens.

It took time for McGovern to win the Forest faithful over. Stranded and miserable at Leeds, especially after Clough's 44 days were up, McGovern would have walked in bare feet, vest and pants down the M1 to get out of there. 'I just got booed before I even made my home debut by the home fans which I found a little bit strange,' he said. He walked into a Forest dressing room containing the nascent talents of John Robertson, Martin O'Neill, Tony Woodcock, Viv Anderson and Ian Bowyer – and got down to the business of creating miracles.

Never the most agile, quick or graceful of players, McGovern did as he was told by Clough and adapted his game to play a more restricted and disciplined role at the base of the midfield, establishing the role while Claude Makelele toddled around in nappies. McGovern was only really interested in securing one man's approval. Speaking to Daniel Taylor in *Deep Into the Forest*, the Scot revealed, 'The fans never took to me wherever I played. I got used to it in the end and it never bothered me because Brian saw things that others didn't and that was all that really mattered.'

He didn't score many goals – that wasn't really his job – but he did score a crucial one in the Nikos Goumas Stadium in Greece to ease his club's passage though to the quarter-finals of the 1978/79 European Cup. Drawing Liverpool in the first round denied McGovern and his team-mates an adventure abroad but having disposed of the reigning European champions, Forest faced AEK Athens in the next round.

Under the tutelage of one of the greatest footballers of all time, Ferenc Puskas, AEK were something of an unknown quantity. 'They weren't one of the strongest sides. The problem we had when we first went in was that we drew Liverpool so we knocked them out. But we still didn't know what the opposition were like – the top teams in Europe,' said McGovern.

Garry Birtles scored Forest's first competitive goal on European soil after sterling work from Frank Clark, who for possibly the only time in his career found himself further up the pitch than John Robertson. Nerves settled, McGovern bundled in a cross from Tony Woodcock. He recalled, 'I half anticipated, because of the move, that the ball might end up where it did. I'm not a natural striker but I do have a football brain. I know that if you're static and the ball comes into the penalty area, very rarely will you score a goal. Most goals are scored by people that are actually moving to get in front of or above someone else.'

Unfazed by finding himself so far forward, he had confidence in not just his own ability but also that of the players around him.

He said, 'I'd gauged it all in my mind. Because of the space that we had the ball in the wide position to start with and the time we had, it wouldn't be the case that they could take it off us and attack us immediately. Once the ball comes into the box, even if it's headed out, I can run back and get back into my position.'

Even if the return leg did turn out to be something of a walk in the park with Forest hammering AEK 5-1, the first leg was anything but. Regarding the game, John Lawson wrote in the *Nottingham Evening Post*, 'The Reds faced everything – a hostile crowd, intimidatory tackling and an appalling penalty decision – to bring back a vital lead to the City Ground.'

McGovern was supremely and rightly confident of progress: 'We were always going to beat AEK Athens down here anyway.'

Forest progressed through to the final and saw off Swedish champions Malmö FF in Munich and the boy from Bo'ness lifted the greatest club prize there is.

'My dad died when I was 11,' McGovern recalled in Jonny Owen's film, *I Believe In Miracles*. 'He never saw me play football. When I received the cup, people say I wasn't smiling. I was kind of smiling but wasn't really over-joyous. That was the first thing that came into my head – I wish my dad was here.'

A year later, McGovern went and lifted the same trophy again at the Santiago Bernabéu Stadium.

Remaining at the club until 1982, McGovern eventually entered the management game, tasting Wembley success by guiding Rotherham United to success in the Auto Windscreens Shield alongside his old pal Archie Gemmill. Although no European Cup, such success gave him plenty of satisfaction.

Of that success, he said, 'I didn't appreciate that the feeling when you've won at Wembley is even greater when you're part of a management team than as a player. Although I'm only saying that because I had won there as a player, you win at Wembley, it's fantastic but you win at Wembley as a manager, it's your product that has gone out there in that sense.'

Quite how such a decorated player under Clough was never awarded a cap for his country remains one of football's biggest mysteries.

It was McGovern's tenacity and willingness to do the things that generally went unnoticed that earned him Clough's respect.

Like Kenny Burns says, 'The one that always makes me laugh was John McGovern when he was up against Graeme Souness. Souness used to batter him and knock him down but John McGovern would get back up like a weebly-wobbly thing: just pop back up again. I think he just broke Souness in two, as if he thought, "Och, I'm fed up."'

John McGovern – the rudder in Brian Clough's miraculous team.

Ian Bowyer vs FC Köln (1979)

IT is rare to move into a new home and keep anything that the previous inhabitants have left behind. It's natural to want to start afresh and even if a perfectly serviceable chair remains in the corner of the living room – left as a token of goodwill or more likely, because the sellers couldn't quite see where it might fit into their own hew home – it will probably, at best, remain unused and unloved – an ever-present reminder that other people lived here before you.

When Brian Clough swept into the City Ground in January 1975, he had decisions to make. He needed to identify which players he could work with and which could be jettisoned. Some of the old furniture needed to be chucked but he was canny enough to realise that he had inherited five of the finest and comfiest chairs he would ever have the pleasure to sit on: John Robertson, Martin O'Neill, Viv Anderson, Tony Woodcock and Ian Bowyer.

The last name in this celebrated merry band of five is often overlooked. Yet Bowyer went on to play 564 games for the club (most of them under Clough) between 1973 and 1987 – punctuated by a very brief spell at Sunderland but hastily brought back since Clough realised he had dropped a clanger in letting him leave as part of his dismantling of his all-conquering side.

Bowyer started his career in the week after England won the World Cup, as an apprentice with Manchester City. He developed a name for himself as a goalscoring midfielder for City and Leyton Orient before ending up at the nice and middling club that was Nottingham Forest.

Two years after Bowyer arrived, Clough rocked up and things started to happen. Bowyer effectively grabbed his exam paper from the middle of the pile and slapped it on the top with a goal to make Lionel Messi jealous by scoring one of his brace in a 4-3 victory against Hereford in the promotion season of 1976/77. Deep inside his own half, he bamboozled two opposition midfielders before winning a crunching tackle and powered towards the goal. By the time the ball nestled in the Bridgford End net, five players had been comprehensively beaten and sat on their arses looking bereft and glum.

He celebrated by clenching his arm and showing off his guns. Mild-mannered on the outside but a fiercely competitive character on the pitch, in *I Believe In Miracles*, Daniel Taylor describes him as 'future captain material brought up on hard graft and discipline, driving an unpretentious Ford Capri – "two-tone: brown and rust" – already at 23, an important voice in the dressing room. He had a useful knack of scoring important goals and he was fearless in the tackle.'

And so the rise to greatness began. Promotion. Titles. League Cups. And then the big one: the European Cup. Not many players score in both legs of a European Cup semi-final – well, not unless you are Cristiano Ronaldo – and certainly not many midfielders, but Bowyer did.

The first leg against FC Köln is regarded as one of the greatest nights at the City Ground. The fact that the game ended 3-3 tells only a tiny morsel of the story. Forest were two goals down and overrun before Birtles pulled a goal back with a looping header. This comeback wasn't done yet though and Bowyer restored parity with a crisp strike from 12 yards. This goal was significant – as demonstrated by Bowyer, this time raising both clenched arms aloft.

That wasn't the end of it though. With 30 minutes remaining, John Robertson stuck his head in among the boots to nod Forest into the lead. Comeback complete. Except it wasn't as Peter Shilton allowed Yasuhiko Okudera's speculative shot to squirm under his bear-like frame for 3-3.

Cue headlines referencing Japanese subs. Cue Brian addressing the watching audience on television sporting quite possibly the warmest brown jumper that ever existed with that cheeky and knowing glint in his eyes, 'I hope anybody's not stupid enough to write us off.'

Just one goal was required. No big deal. Just a goal and to keep a clean sheet in the intimidating Müngersdorfer Stadion against the reigning German champions who had just stuck three goals past Forest on their own turf. That's all – nothing more, nothing less.

With so much at stake, it was a predictably tight game. Given the concession of three away goals, Forest dared not concede another yet at the same time needed to attack in order to tip the balance of the scoreline in their favour.

By the 65th minute, all was going to plan. The FC Köln attack had been stifled and Raymond van Gool – such a thorn in the side of the Forest defence in the first leg – was nullified.

In the blink of an eye, Robertson was released down the left until a sliding tackle robbed him of possession. The ball spun away for a corner. John McGovern was, as usual, anchoring the midfield.

Bowyer recalled, 'It's a well-crafted goal. You've got a genius chipping it into the near post, and you've got Garry Birtles just getting there with the deftest of touches.

'But they can go wrong just like that: he can head it too well, he can head it up in the air and the keeper will come and get it, he can mis-head it.'

But Bowyer was on the move because he was a midfield player; he was not a centre-half that the opposition were going to worry about.

He continued, 'Once we scored, I wouldn't say we were "comfortable" comfortable, but we certainly did enough to deserve to go through.'

Typically self-effacing, Bowyer himself simply stated about the goal, 'I headed the thing into the net.'

⚽⚽⚽

As the ball hits the net, eluding a body on the line, a Köln defender has his head in his hands. He knows. His mates mob Bowyer. He isn't able to perform his customary celebration until they've released him. Once they do, almost to himself, he raises his arms and punches the air. Nothing flashy: just satisfaction in the job getting done with the minimum of fuss. A European Cup Final awaits. Actually, a couple of European Cup winner's medals await.

❂ ❂ ❂

The goal changed lives, including that of the recent £1m player and future European Cup Final scorer, Trevor Francis. 'I'll never forget that header from Ian Bowyer,' he says. 'When I look back, there are certain moments and certain players who indirectly played a significant part in my footballing career.

Ian Bowyer was one and I've got a lot to thank him for because it gave me the chance to have the opportunity of playing in the final.'

Yet the comedown is always the worst part. By May 1980, Clough got busy refreshing his team. In retrospect, he burnt it to the ground too quickly, something he freely admitted in later years. Rather than pouring lighter fuel all over his team, maybe lighting a few scented tea-candles here and there would have made for an easier transition into the 80s.

Tony Woodcock and Archie Gemmill had already been gone for a year but following them through the doors in the months after the reclamation of the European Cup were Garry Birtles, Martin O'Neill, Larry Lloyd and Bowyer. The backbone of the team was gone. Give it just one more year and Kenny Burns, Trevor Francis and John McGovern would be gone too. By 1982, only Viv Anderson, Peter Shilton and John Robertson remained from the starting line-up for the 1979 European Cup Final. That's more churn than a 'cream into butter' factory.

Perhaps realising his haste, Clough set about patching the team back together again with glue, paper clips and used chewing gum. Bowyer was recalled to the City Ground after only 15 appearances for Sunderland.

Clough had a plan and Bowyer was a central cog in it. He shook himself down and set about tackling arguably the biggest challenge of his managerial career. He could have walked away but instead knuckled down with an eye on balancing the books and building one last great team.

By the summer of 1983, Forest finished a very respectable fifth in the table and things were starting to settle down a little. Birtles was back by now – pride severely dented after an unsatisfactory spell with Manchester United – and the whole Justin Fashanu experiment was old news as he was sold to Notts County after being farmed out on loan to Southampton. Experience in the form of Colin Todd arrived alongside Paul Hart and Hans van Breukelen. The bill for the Executive Stand was down to £1m with an overdraft of £800,000. Not perfect but better.

All the while, Bowyer continued to do what he'd always done: grafted in the middle of the park, offering words of wisdom to young charges such as Steve Hodge and Chris Fairclough while still popping up with the odd crucial goal.

Yet events beyond even Brian Clough conspired against him. In 1983, gate-sharing was dispensed with. No longer would the away club receive 20 per cent of the revenue from attendance. For Forest, this was yet another barrier to overcome in order to maintain pace with the elite clubs. The trophy cabinet suggests they were indeed an elite club but season ticket sales, attendances and the bank manager strongly implied otherwise.

Against such a testing backdrop, Clough turned in a beautifully rounded pebble of a season in 1983/84. He came out fighting and landed a few well-placed haymakers. The mojo was stirring. The UEFA Cup run of that year suggested Clough hadn't quite given up on continental glory just yet. A 0-0 home tie against Celtic in the third round on a frozen pitch had most commentators writing off Forest's chances of progression. Fools. Piteous fools.

Clough's young Forest side went and chalked up a 2-1 win at Celtic Park while a partisan 68,000 crowd bayed for blood. They got none from Clough's young team, guided by the irrepressible Bowyer cajoling and encouraging the young charges around him while sticking in a crunching tackle once in a while.

Then RSC Anderlecht happened. RSC Anderlecht and a dodgy referee put paid to Clough and Bowyer tasting further European glory.

Nonetheless, the team finished strongly, winning their last three games of the season and banging in a division-high 76 goals to claim third in the league (only six points behind champions Liverpool), and they also reached the UEFA Cup semi-finals (only denied a final by later proven corruption). In fact, were it not for a wretched February and March in which Forest dropped points in the last minute of four games, another title might well have been in the cabinet.

Bowyer was the heartbeat and moral anchor of a team that would, after his release in 1987, evolve into Clough's young and neatly coiffed men with straight backs who didn't argue with referees and were once again close to maintaining their status as the neutral's favourite.

Mr Nottingham Forest, Bowyer pretty much played in every position for the club, including in goal – not just once, but twice.

When regular number one John Middleton got injured against Oxford United, Bowyer helped his team to a 1-0 win in 1975. In 1986, he was at it again against Leicester City. Steve Sutton picked up an injury just before half-time and once again, Bowyer stepped in and incredibly, saved a penalty from Gary McAllister.

Sadly for Forest and Bowyer, the referee ordered a re-take on the basis that Bowyer had moved too soon. Not to be denied, Bowyer saved from McAllister again yet the Scot quickly latched on to the rebound and deposited both the ball and Bowyer into the net. Leicester ran out 3-1 winners and although the record books don't record Bowyer saving a penalty or two, technically speaking, he did precisely that.

As Bowyer prepared to play a game in his final season – a 1-0 win against Everton shown live on television in January of 1987 – Clough said of him, 'He's nearly become a friend.' At the heart of much of the success at Nottingham Forest were Brian Clough and Ian Bowyer – two 'nearly' friends.

Asked about his status and significance to Forest, Bowyer is typically reticent to bang his own drum. 'Legend? Everybody's a legend these days. That's for other people to decide.'

The folk of the red half of Nottingham decided. Legend he most definitely is.

Trevor Francis vs Malmö FF (1979)

O N the day that Trevor Francis was unveiled as football's first million-pound player, the question of whether he was indeed worth it was diminished to the very distant recesses of the minds of those watching by a quite brilliant and eclectic number of factors.

To start with, Trevor and his wife Helen rolled up in the most magnificently avocado-coloured Audi to the Main Stand at the City Ground. Helen elegantly stepped out sporting a fur coat that appeared to be in the process of spawning numerous other fluffy fur coats of its own.

Then there was the width of Trevor's tie – lurching across his chest like the Artemision Bronze statue depicting Zeus or Poseidon (no one seems to be able to decide) with arms and legs wide and glorious.

The crowning glory – the showstopper – the gleaming red cherry resplendent atop a particularly scrumptious cake – was Brian Clough's shiny red jacket. It was as if he had borrowed a lovely bit of kit from a NASA astronaut and sprayed it vibrant and lustrous red with an industrial-sized tin of noxious spray paint.

A reporter asked Francis, flanked by Peter Taylor and Clough, when he expected to play his first game for Forest.

'When I pick him,' Clough interjected, leaving Francis with his mouth half-open.

And with that, Francis and the watching world were reminded that for all the hullabaloo, razzamatazz and chutzpah, he was a footballer who would be paid to play football and would play when Clough felt he could make a contribution. End of story.

Moreover, Francis's future team-mates could rest easy knowing that their gaffer had faith in what they had achieved so far and that Francis's ego would not require a dressing room of its own.

As it was, Francis was never the type to require bringing down a peg or two. He was no bad boy with vices who would need taming by Clough and Taylor. Far from it. In *With Clough by Taylor*, Taylor recalls how, 'Trevor deadlocked with us over Detroit, yet in a most deferential way, addressing us as "Mr Clough" and "Mr Taylor" when talking terms and continually consulting a list of sensible questions compiled with the help of his wife.

'He was so polite and well-mannered that we almost moderated our usual lay-it-on-the-line and give-'em-hell approach to new signings.'

Signing him was far from straightforward. Coventry City offered a more lucrative contract than Forest but he didn't hand in a transfer request at Birmingham for more money – he wanted silverware and to play with better quality players and to play under 'the great man himself'.

The situation was complicated further by him spending the close season with Detroit Express. At the time Jimmy Hill had a complicated tie-in deal with the emerging American club and lured Francis out to play in the States during the close season. He picked up a groin injury early on yet being desperate to please and rather than sit on the sidelines, he played through the pain in an effort to justify his more than adequate wages.

Like Taylor said, polite and well-mannered.

On the day of the avocado Audi, fur coat, wide ties and shiny space jackets, Francis was a little surprised to be kept waiting. But wait he must. After all, Brian had a game of squash with Garry Birtles to finish.

The first £1m footballer? The truth is that the actual figure was £1.15m. Birmingham manager Jim Smith pushed for the big one on the basis of trying to nab Chris Woods and youth player Stephen Burke as part of the deal. Forest weren't interested so once the levy had been paid, Francis was indeed the first one-and-a-bit-million-pound player.

'There's the famous story of "I was the million-pound tea boy" and that was Brian. If I wasn't involved in the team – in the early days when I first came here, I was cup-tied on one or two occasions – it was my job and it wasn't a problem to make the guys a cup of tea because they were the guys that were trying to win a game of football,' Francis recalled.

'But of course it got publicised then as "I was the million-pound tea boy" but it didn't bother me; it was all part of him – Brian Clough – trying to generate good spirit. But when you're a successful team, it's not too difficult to create a good dressing room spirit. It's when you're losing week after week that it becomes a problem.'

Francis had seen Clough and his team scooping up trophies for fun and fancied a bit of that himself.

'I came in as the first million-pound footballer and I was a little bit in awe of what I was walking into. There were a lot of big name players here. With respect to what I left at Birmingham City, they weren't the calibre or quality of players. But Brian Clough treated the players and me as just one of the group. There was never any problem because I didn't have any ego at all but it was a bit special coming into this group and Brian – he worked incredibly hard at trying at trying to generate spirit, bringing everybody together.'

After making a debut of sorts under Clough playing for a Forest A-team against Notts County in the Midlands Youth League, Francis made his actual bow at Portman Road against Ipswich Town.

The home crowd was unrelenting in their vocal claim that Francis was a 'waste of money'. In desperation to prove them he was anything but, he punched a cross it into the net out of desperation. Naturally, even without the modern aid of VAR, the goal was disallowed.

The changing room afterwards was halted in its tracks. Clough's voiced ordered them to 'stop what you're doing'. Francis then received what he calls, 'one of the biggest telling-offs I've had in my football career'. No doubt some language more industrial than a Sheffield steel mill in the 19th century was employed but the gist of it was, according to Francis, "'We don't cheat here. Don't ever let that happen again. Get in the shower.'"

Francis had been ineligible to play in Forest's European games prior to the final. Some very difficult decisions regarding the team to face Malmö FF in Munich's Olympiastadion lay ahead. Archie Gemmill and Martin O'Neill had been carrying knocks in the build-up and Francis had no expectation he would start yet he recalls the scene clear as day. He and the team were sat down at 11am on the perimeter track. His name was the 11th one to be read out. He was in.

As others felt the reverberations of the team selection, Francis got on with preparing for the game. He had a lot of emotional baggage on his plate: it would be his European debut and not only did his price tag hover into focus, he felt the pressure of replacing O'Neill and living up to the faith his gaffer had in him.

☻ ☻ ☻

With a tight first half drawing to a close, Ian Bowyer spreads a ball out to John Robertson. At the moment Bowyer does this, Francis is on the halfway line. He looks up and sees the ball at Robbo's feet, which can only mean one thing – get in the box ready for a cross.

Of all the things that Clough has ever said to him, this is rule number one. If you knew that Picasso was in town with a brush in his hand yet you lounged around at home watching your cat take a nap, you deserve nothing more than the life of a dung beetle.

Francis gets on his bike.

☻ ☻ ☻

Robertson suckers two defenders in to him yet just when it looks like he's lost control or slowed to a standstill, he shimmies and shuffles and he's shaping to cross.

✪ ✪ ✪

'When it came in, I made good contact and I was never in doubt that I would hit the target. I wasn't quite so sure that I would beat the goalkeeper because I was more assured when I was kicking the ball with my boot than I was with my head,' recalls the scorer.

✪ ✪ ✪

It's easy to overlook how far wide of the far post Francis is when he makes contact with the ball. It's anything but a far-post-tap in. It's more of a 'strain every sinew in your neck and crane your head further than you ever thought allowable' type header – with added control too.

The ball hits the roof of the net.

✪ ✪ ✪

'My life changed from the moment I got on the end of John Robertson's cross,' Francis admits.

Time slowed down. Being a £1m footballer no longer mattered. In such moments are lifetime achievements forged.

What most people remember then is him tumbling across the discus circle. He recalls, 'I'd like to turn around and say that I was the bravest person in the world but I wasn't because the discus circle was rubber. It would not have made any difference because at that moment, you're on such a high, the adrenaline is flowing and it's on the stroke of half-time and it masked what was a poor first-half performance. We went in a goal up. It probably made the half-time team talk from Brian slightly easier.'

Less than an hour later, Nottingham Forest were champions of Europe and if there was a weight of expectation around

Francis's neck, it lay in tatters on the running track of a stadium in Germany.

But, arguably, Francis's finest performance in a Forest shirt was yet to come. After the disappointment of a disjointed League Cup Final against Wolves in which Andy Gray bundled home after a mix-up between Peter Shilton and David Needham, Forest prepared to travel to Berlin for the quarter-final of the European Cup. They were up against it having made heavy weather of the first leg – losing 1-0. Their grip on the League Cup had finally been shaken free and now it seemed their fingers were being prised off the European Cup too.

A frosty atmosphere permeated preparations for Berlin. Francis felt Clough had blamed him for the Wolves defeat and barely a word was spoken between them since. Practising on the pitch in -13 conditions in deepest, darkest Berlin, Clough uttered his first words to Francis since Wembley:

'Where do you want to play tonight?'

'You know where I want to play boss – up the middle.'

'Start there and make sure you finish there.'

He did exactly that and turned in what he felt was his finest all-round performance for the club.

With only a quarter of an hour gone, Francis bundled in from Needham's flick-on. All square on aggregate. Nerves well and truly settled. Still exceedingly cold though.

On 35 minutes, Francis turned his marker inside out on the corner of the penalty area and smashed the ball into the top corner from an angle of Marco van Basten circa 1988 proportions. It's an astonishing finish, which requires numerous viewings to confirm that yes; he did indeed really just do that. Less cold. Getting warmer.

Just before half-time, Robertson was unfairly felled in the box and he calmly slotted home the resulting penalty. Forest were into the semi-finals of the European Cup. Again. T-shirt weather.

But before Forest were able to see off Ajax to confirm another final and successfully defend their status as European champions, things went south for Francis. Despite cruising to a 4-0 win against Crystal Palace, he pushed to complete a hat-trick and in doing so felt a tight pain in the back of his leg. He didn't know it at the time but his Achilles tendon was ruptured, meaning he would miss out not only on Forest's victory in Madrid but also the European Championships in Italy.

Birtles would run himself into the ground while Robertson plundered the winning goal yet from the moment McGovern lifted the trophy (again) in the Estadio Santiago Bernabéu, it felt like the start of the end of an era.

Like so many key players of the miracle years, and although Francis was included in the promotional material for the forthcoming 1981/82 season – which started with him scoring two goals in a 2-1 win against Southampton, featured on *Match of the Day* – Clough decided to sell him.

Maybe Clough wasn't totally convinced of Francis's ability to fully recover from his injury. Maybe Francis himself had grown weary of Clough's treatment of him – in *Nobody Ever Says Thank You*, Jonathon Wilson tells of how in the European Cup game away to Östers IF, he had to find a public toilet to use because Clough wouldn't allow him in the dressing room while he was speaking.

Maybe the construction of the new Executive Stand (later named the Brian Clough Stand) was eating away at the club's finances and given Francis's contract expired at the end of the season, shipping him out made sound financial sense. Maybe, like so many other players at this time, Clough simply felt that it was time to scorch his all-conquering team to the ground and build anther one.

Eventually he was sold to Manchester City for £1.2m. Francis made 93 appearances for Forest, scoring 37 goals – a scoring rate similar to that of Kylian Mbappé after his first season at AS Monaco but with a European Cup Final winner chucked in just for good measure. Never mind £1m, it begs the question what Francis would go for in the current market.

Francis freely admits that the goal in Munich, which sealed Forest's first European Cup, was the most important goal in his career. When asked if it was the most important goal in Nottingham Forest's history, he pauses. He's never been asked before. Eventually he tentatively agrees that yes, yes it is. Achieving something for the first time is always the hardest thing to do.

Being the first £1m player is quite a billing to live up to yet he paid that debt in full and with added interest.

John Robertson vs Hamburger SV (1980)

WHEN Brian Clough blustered his way into Nottingham on 6 January 1975, a young Scot by the name of John Robertson was flailing around in the reserves after leaving his native Scotland in the summer of 1968 at the age of 15. Just five years later, that young Scotsman had won pretty much everything there is to win in the game. Brian Clough recognised a genius when he saw one.

Once Clough and Peter Taylor had picked him up, shook him down and turned him into something new, there was no stopping him – he was on his way to being voted number one in the club's top 50 players of all time.

It was in the European Cup Final of 1979 that Robertson would make the most telling of contributions. As Barry Davies famously said in commentary after he swung across a sumptuous cross for Trevor Francis to head into the roof of the net before scraping his knees on a Bavarian discus circle, 'That's what I've wanted to see him do.' But it's not as if Robertson was stood around on the left wing indulging himself in some chin stroking while deep in existentialist thought and smoking a Gitanes up until that point.

Each time he received the ball, he found two sky blue shirts swarm around him. Nowhere is this more evident than in the build-up for the goal. He receives the ball still relatively deep and as he makes inroads into the Malmö half, two defenders converge on him. They know what he's capable of delivering. Cutting inside is not really on – he's going to have to go outside.

He shapes to do exactly this and for one split second, he seems to get the ball stuck under his feet but just as quickly, he pokes it further down the line. One touch, two touches and he's gone. The Swedish defenders had him but somehow, they've been beaten for pace by the lad with the chip-fat smile. But the cross... oh, the cross. There's really only one space into which he can deliver the ball in order to give Francis a chance. No matter, he does exactly that.

Francis himself is happy to acknowledge Robertson's contribution to this iconic goal, 'It was always my responsibility to get to the back post whenever John Robertson was in possession because John was – I use the term genius with regard to Brian Clough – and John wasn't far behind that, he was an exceptionally talented left-sided player who didn't quite receive the acclaim that he merited.

'He was our best player and whenever he had possession, nine times out of ten he would get past the full-back and deliver balls from the byline so I had to get there because I knew that that ball was coming.'

A year later, Robertson surpassed this and went and scored the winner in a European Cup Final. Take a seat and think about that for a minute. In consecutive European Cup finals, he created the winner and then scored it the following year. That's some achievement: one that has gone largely unnoticed beyond Nottingham. No awards. No Ballon d'Or (Kevin Keegan won it in 1979 and Karl-Heinz Rummenigge in 1980). The football world largely shrugged its shoulders while Clough and Taylor's collection of rag-tags and bobtails were crowned Kings of Europe.

It is precisely this collective yawn and looking the other way at the achievement of this Nottingham Forest team that inspired actor and director Jonny Owen to set about recalibrating the balance by making his feature-length film, *I Believe In Miracles*: 'This is very important to me. John Robertson won something like, out of 17 games, he won 15 man of the match awards, scored the winner in one cup final, produced the assist in the other. He wasn't even shortlisted for European Player of the Year. And he was the star player in a back-to-back European Cup-winning team.'

But anyone who might have suggested to Robertson that he would produce such magic a mere four years previous to events in Munich's Olympiastadion would have been dragged through the nettles and dog muck that littered the banks of the River Trent and chucked into the murky water before being unceremoniously bundled back out again and carted off to the type of building in which Brad Pitt's character in *Twelve Monkeys* resides when introduced to Bruce Willis's James Cole.

When Clough first breezed into Nottingham, Robertson wasn't pulling up any trees. He spoke to the *Herald Scotland* in this excellent interview back in 2012, 'When he first came, I wasn't doing the best for myself. I was languishing, feeling sorry for myself. Then when Peter [Taylor] came, he pulled me apart when we were in Germany. The gaffer said Pete was going to have a word. The first thing he [Taylor] said was "You!"'

'I wasn't sure if he was pointing at me or not. But I soon found out. "You eff off back to the hotel!" I was dumbfounded. He said he'd speak to me later. I was to wait by the pool. So I just got up and worried my way back to the hotel. Later, he asked me what my problem was. I said I didn't know what he meant. He said, "I watched you last night in the warm-up and you did three stretches of one groin and three of the other. You stood around. You're overweight, you're scruffy, so again, what's your problem?"'

In short, his problem was that nobody had really believed in him until Clough and Taylor clapped their eyes on him. From then on, he started to blossom and the trademark Robertson movement started to surface – stride around nonchalantly out on the left wing, allow one or two defenders to close him down, somehow squirm away from them before planting the ball into the net. Simple really.

In January 1978 he scored a beauty of a goal against Manchester City in the fourth round of the FA Cup and such movement was becoming a bit of a trademark by now. In

November of that same year, the rightly venerated Brian Moore described a Robertson goal against Tottenham Hotspur as a 'virtuoso piece of wing play' after Robbo gave Spurs full-back Peter Naylor a full-on and dangerous dose of twisted blood. It's really no wonder that Malmö tried to shackle and bind him to the touchline in the final but all he needed was one tiny spyhole of an opening.

But his crowning glory and defining moment is surely the goal that retained the European Cup in 1980 – a feat shared only by Real Madrid, Liverpool and a bunch of chancers from the East Midlands.

⚽ ⚽ ⚽

It starts as most Robertson goals do – wide out left. He ambles slowly but menacingly, closely tracked by Manfred Kaltz. The German, who made 581 appearances for Hamburg – the second highest number in Bundesliga history – was no mug. He denies Robertson the opportunity to go down the outside like he did against Malmö FF a year previously. No way is he going to fall for that one. Not today. Not on his watch.

So Robertson – genuinely two-footed – heads inside towards the goal. He lays the ball in to Garry Birtles but he's crowded out and so nearly loses possession. Just when it seems that the ball is lost, Birtles scoops it back to Robertson in a fashion reminiscent to that of Mario Balotelli when he produced his one and only assist of the season to set up Sergio Agüero 32 years later to score one of the most dramatic goals ever on English soil. There is nothing too remarkable about this apart from the fact that Birtles is on his arse when he does so.

Meanwhile, Robertson has continued to move forward. With his team-mate languishing on the Spanish soil, he checks his run but when Birtles's leg telescopes out to retrieve the ball, he's off again. He smuggles ball away from the feet of Kevin Keegan – a most satisfying element in the build-up to this goal – and finds himself on the edge of the penalty box. In that very moment though, he is unaware that Keegan is close by, only realising this when he saw it back on television.

It seems like space for a shot is at a premium. Three defenders bear down on him and team-mate Gary Mills is shaping to steal the ball for a shot of his own. Besides, Robertson is still 14 yards out so any shot is going to have to be taken quickly and accurately if it is to evade the grasp of Rudolf Kargus.

Robertson doesn't seem composed or set for his shot at the moment of release. It is low and carefully struck rather than blasted with hope and a prayer. But it's enough, especially since Kargus has taken a step to set himself at just the wrong moment. Rarely has a ball nestled so sweetly into the corner of a net.

⚽ ⚽ ⚽

The details are still very much lodged in the great man's mind, 'Gary Mills picked it up in the middle of the field and tried to play a ball and it broke back to me about halfway inside their half. Mannie Kaltz was the right-back and he tried to come and confront me. I took it inside of him, played the ball to Birtles – who did unbelievably well because it wasn't the best ball I gave to him – he worked a miracle to get it back to me. I took a touch and fired in and fortunately it went into the net.'

⚽ ⚽ ⚽

He stands, both arms aloft and remains so while mobbed by his mates. And they are his mates. He drinks with them. He goes on to remain close friends with them – most notably Martin O'Neill and Larry Lloyd. He doesn't know it but he's only gone and scored the goal that will secure him and his mates another European Cup.

Rather beautifully, Viv Anderson simply gives him a brief pat on the head as if to indicate that it's just another Robbo goal – it's just what he does. In many ways, Viv is right – this is just what Robbo does: he provides assists for European Cup winning goals and scores European Cup winning goals. Robbo's own thoughts? A very understated, 'It was great – a fantastic feeling.'

☺ ☺ ☺

With so many achievements to choose from, rather predictably, Robertson finds it difficult to specify one thing that gives him the most pleasure. As befitting such a humble gentleman, he takes special pride in winning the league and going 42 games unbeaten. The influence of Clough and Taylor is deep with this one, nowhere more clearly evident than in footage of an interview with him just after his decisive penalty secured Forest the League Cup in 1978 after a replay against Liverpool.

In the post-match interview, the young Robbo skulks around in the background like a naughty schoolboy having been caught with a fag in his hand behind the bike sheds before being brought forward by the paternal arm of Taylor. Taylor pulls him closer to him in an act of both gratitude and protection from the brickbats regarding the awarding of the controversial spot kick. Taylor and Clough bloody loved this lad.

His demeanour didn't change. That carefree nonchalance off the pitch continued as Stuart Pearce testifies in his autobiography, 'We were all together on the ten-day pre-season tour of the south coast with the colourful John Robertson immediately earning cult status among the new boys by turning up with a toothbrush in his back pocket and no clothes other than those he stood in.'

He's still the same now – rocking up to be honoured at a film festival in Bilbao with only a passport, toothbrush and the clothes on his back. Yet don't be fooled by this shambolic exterior since beneath it lies a perceptive footballing brain. In *Tackling My Demons*, Stan Collymore recognised what lay beneath while playing under him and Martin O'Neill at Leicester City, 'Next thing, John "Robbo" Robertson, Martin's number two, came out to watch. He had a fag in his mouth, too,' Collymore recalls.

'Robbo always wore a suit, but his tie was invariably halfway down his shirt, and he chain-smoked. He would just stand on the touchline, calling out "well done, son" or "brilliant, son". Nothing negative. Ever. If he wanted to give you a bit of advice, he would come across when the session was over and put his arm around you while you were walking off. And even on that first day, I suddenly began to realise where Leicester had built all their spirit from.'

Just reading Collymore's description of Robbo makes you wish he was your Sunday league or five-a-side coach. Clearly, Robbo understands footballers and what makes them tick.

His contribution to this golden period in the history of Nottingham Forest cannot be underestimated. His captain, John McGovern, told *The Guardian*, 'When I try to tell people how good he was it can be difficult because it was over 30 years ago. So what I generally say is: You know a few years ago there was a guy called Ryan Giggs who played until he was 40 and was regarded as one of the best left-wingers of all time? Well, John Robertson was like Ryan Giggs but with two good feet, not one.'

As far as the modern game goes, Robertson rates the snake-hipped Lionel Messi highly and naturally, loves the way he can unpick even the tightest defence, even when opposition teams tend to line up in an ultra-defensive formation against Barcelona.

An aspect of football that clearly irks Robertson is the nitpicking nature of modern punditry that focuses on defensive frailties. From his perspective, a goal is generally the consequence of a piece of creativity, rather than a defensive error. It is all too easy to reprimand a defender for not being in the right place or getting dragged out of position: more often than not, this is borne out of the necessity to react to the opposite number's movement or piece of skill.

It's fair to say that the fast forward icon on the remote control is no longer visible due to being particularly well-thumbed, reaching peak use around 10.45pm on a Saturday. And don't even get him started on the modern player's inability to ride a tackle.

Clough and Taylor built their miracle team around this short, unfit and scruffy lad who lacked pace and strength. But the composition of genius is a complicated business and whatever he lacked, Robertson was a genius with the ball. Of all the Nottingham Forest History Boys, Robertson remains the most significant and artistic of them all.

Steve Hodge vs
RSC Anderlecht (1984)

STEVE Hodge almost definitely doesn't buy Belgian beer or chocolates, especially if their origin is a district in the south west of Brussels. In the space of 14 days, RSC Anderlecht provided Hodge with his finest moment as a footballer, closely followed by his lowest.

Although Tommy Gemmell arrived from Celtic for the 1971/72 season, Ian Storey-Moore left for Manchester United, and Nottingham Forest, after three seasons scratching around the lower reaches of the First Division, slipped to 21st and were relegated.

Watching from the East Stand that season was a grandfather, a father and a son. They would travel in from nearby Gedling – around five miles from the City Ground – for each game. Sometimes, the father would hoist the son on to his shoulders; on other occasions, the son would stand at the front on an upturned milk crate. Regardless, the young nine-year-old son would stare in awe at the players. One day, he thought, one day.

Ten years later, Hodge would emulate his boyhood heroes by slipping on a first team shirt at Ipswich Town's Portman Road. It mattered not that it was the final game of the season – this was a game against the runners-up boasting a fine team: Hodge can still reel off the classy players he lined up against that day.

At 1.50pm, Brian Clough told the nervous young lad who grew up watching Forest to put the number nine shirt on as he was playing centre-forward that day. Although he could play in that position, Hodge wasn't really a centre-forward and besides, he was very short – Mick Mills and Terry Butcher could quite feasibly have scooped him up and stuffed him down their socks. Yet perhaps Clough recalled that moment four years previously at this very ground when he told his left-back who had never scored a goal in his long career to go and play centre-forward. He did just that and Frank Clark scored the only goal of his career. Portman Road was a good ground for makeshift strikers playing for Nottingham Forest.

As usual, Clough was right – strike partner Peter Davenport scored a hat-trick and Forest won 3-1. Hodge set up a goal for Davenport and was then subbed: he had spent the afternoon running around like a lunatic and was, frankly, knackered. Indeed, after being substituted, Clough undid his laces for him on the bench in a very public gesture of recognition for his efforts. Forest finished in an underwhelming 12th position.

The following season started well. Although they were well beaten at home by Manchester United, this was sandwiched between wins against West Ham United and Brighton & Hove Albion. Next up was Liverpool at Anfield: reigning domestic champions, and by the end of the season they retained the trophy. Although Forest lost 4-3 owing to a last-minute Ian Rush winner, Hodge bagged two goals and started to feel he could cut it as a professional footballer. Scoring two goals at Anfield tends to give you a bit of confidence.

Hodge was surrounded by good company and was learning from not only Brian Clough but a man who had won a lot of trinkets in his time at Forest. 'Ian Bowyer was my mentor,' he told NFFCTube. 'I learned so much from him for years.'

Fifth position in the league at the end of this season meant European football back then. Progress to the third round of the 1983/84 UEFA Cup was smooth and then Celtic came out of the pot. The first-leg tie at the City Ground was a strangely eventful evening for a goalless draw. Freezing conditions meant the pitch was frozen yet with seemingly half of Glasgow having descended on Nottingham for the game, postponing it was, in those days, a non-starter.

The City Ground was bursting at the seams, especially in the away end and at one stage, play was interrupted as fans spilled on to the pitch to momentarily escape the crush. In retrospect, perhaps the game shouldn't have been played.

In footballing terms though, Clough was happy with the clean sheet. He told his players before the game, 'I'm not bothered about anything else tonight – all I want is no goals against.' He had his wish.

Few gave Forest much of a chance of progression given they had to get a result at Celtic Park in front of 68,000 baying fans. Clough knew European football better than his inside leg measurements though and his dynamic young team turned in a perfect performance. The game was goalless at half-time until Hodge opened the scoring early in the second half.

It was a masterclass of an away goal too – Steve Wigley tore down the right, utterly ignorant of the Jungle's taunts, and crossed to Davenport who held the ball up, turned and laid the ball on a silver platter for the onrushing Hodge, bursting from midfield and planting the ball beyond Packie Bonner into the corner of the net before David Platt and Frank Lampard even knew what a goalscoring midfielder was.

The second goal, converted by Colin Walsh after more fine work by Davenport, nailed the coffin door firmly on to Celtic's European journey. Forest squeezed past SK Sturm Graz in the next round and then found themselves up against RSC Anderlecht in the semi-final.

Anderlecht. Like 'Yeovil', it is a word that is the catalyst for a tumultuous swirl of emotions for Nottingham Forest fans. If the mere utterance of 'Yeovil' prompts a severe bout of existential despair, 'Anderlecht' elicits, at best, a sad shake of the head yet more likely, a sustained and possibly violent display of anger and bitterness.

The first leg proved to be Hodge's nirvana. Goalless after 84 minutes, Hodge happened. The game itself was a cracking affair. Gary Mills should have opened the scoring early on when put clean through but nudged his effort inches wide of the post.

Peter Davenport had an effort cleared off the line while at the other end, Enzo Scifo let rip with a shot from a flicked free kick that required urgent action from Hans van Breukelen.

As the game came to a climax, Forest forced a flurry of corners. After Mills's corner was cleared, the ball came back to him so he launched an inviting cross to the far post where Hodge nodded in to notch a vital goal. He wasn't done yet though. Four minutes later, Wigley found space down the right and crossed for Hodge to dive acrobatically and guide the ball into the Trent End net. Two headers in the space of four minutes from one of the smallest players on the field. Football, eh?

'I scored two down here in the last ten minutes of the semi-final – two headers at the Trent End – the second of which was the best goal I ever scored in my career – a diving header and we thought that probably would be enough,' Hodge reflected.

It should have been enough. It *was* enough, or at least it was were it not the case that something very underhand and wrong was lurking round the corner.

Something was in the air as the team walked out to defend their two-goal lead with a view to nicking one more, just to be sure. That something was a poisonous atmosphere. Those fans present that evening speak of feeling afraid as they were penned into a tight corner of the ground, missiles raining in from all angles.

On the pitch, Forest were up against a team packed with talent, most notably Scifo, who would lead his country to the semi-finals of the World Cup in Mexico just two years later.

The home crowd grew restless. The away fans were jammed into a fenced paddock. Something was wrong, very wrong.

'On the night, Scifo scored in the first half – great goal. Can't stop that; he's a talented boy. The second was a penalty – a guy called Kenneth Brylle. He's dived and I was two yards from where Kenny Swain was,' said Hodge.

It was a penalty waiting to happen but not in the way you think. Brylle burst past Swain and then his legs simply buckled under him. Swain was a yard away and the referee fell for it. Paul Hart, playing in defence for Forest that evening, corroborates

Hodge's account. 'Kenny must have been three yards away,' Hart told Daniel Taylor for *The Guardian*. 'It was a blatant dive anyway. But I can't stress this enough, Kenny was a mile off him. It could easily have been offside as well.'

It got worse in the 88th minute. 'And then they get the third goal. A lad called Erwin Vandenbergh [six times the top scorer in the Belgian First Division], played for Belgium. Great striker,' said Hodge.

One could be forgiven for thinking at this stage that Forest had only themselves to blame for frittering away a two-goal lead. And up to a point, that's fair. Penalties happen; some harsh, some fair and even if on this occasion, the penalty awarded was exceptionally harsh on Forest, well, that's football. Yet when Hart nodded Forest's vital away goal in injury time, only for it to be disallowed, well something seemed to be very rotten.

Hart rose in the penalty area to meet the corner kick from Walsh. His arms weren't raised in order to gain an advantage; he just jumped the highest. The ball somehow eluded the Belgian defence and ended up in the net. It didn't matter though. It was destined to be a futile gesture.

'My head had gone by then,' admits Hodge. 'I'd been booked – and Cloughie had took me off. I was on the bench. The corner went in and I heard a whistle immediately from the referee, as soon as that kick was taken.

'For a moment, it was bedlam on our bench and everyone was up. I didn't move. I'd heard it – straightaway when it was kicked. The referee was never going to allow any possibility that the corner would result in a header from one of our players. His job was done by then.'

Hart, unaware of any whistle, maintains his innocence, 'I headed it as clean as a whistle. The ball flew past Ian Bowyer and into the net and that would have been us in the final. Their goalkeeper was already berating his defenders, and then the whistle went. Nobody had a clue why. I said to Ian, "Were you offside? Did you push someone?" He said, "Don't be silly." But it was disallowed.'

Garry Birtles shares Hodge's despondency and dreadful feeling that something wasn't right. 'Colin Walsh put over the corner and it was more or less a free header,' he told *The Guardian*. 'There was no contact with a defender whatsoever. We were just looking at each other thinking, "What on earth is going on here?" It was embarrassing. Your natural thought is not that it was a bent referee, but we knew we'd been done.'

The Belgian commentator was as confused as anyone, emitting a chuckle in surprise following an actual, 'ooh-la-la'. He couldn't quite believe it either, and neither could the UEFA delegate.

'The final whistle goes and we're in the changing room,' Hodge recounts. 'We were followed by a Korean fellow, a UEFA official who goes with every team. I remember him saying to Brian Clough after in the dressing room, "Mister Clough, I think you've got grounds for complaint tonight." And that's a UEFA official. Clough just said, "Young man, I've not complained about a referee in 20 years; I'm not going to start now."'

On the final whistle, van Breukelen kicked the ball towards the referee from around 30 yards away – only just missing him.

The truth finally emerged in 1997 when the Belgian club admitted that their former president, Constant Vanden Stock, had used a local gangster to pay the Spanish referee that evening, Emilio Guruceta Muro, £18,000. Muro would die in a car accident in 1987. To this day, RSC Anderlecht play in the Constant Vanden Stock Stadium.

It is an episode in the history of Nottingham Forest that still hurts and probably always will. 'On a football pitch, where sometimes people will try things and get away with it, then I can accept that to a certain degree,' Hodge states. 'But I can't accept people being bribed. I can't have any sympathy at all to Anderlecht, even now to this day.'

It is precisely this episode that leaves the biggest scar on Hodge's successful career, 'I've played in a World Cup quarter-final and lost to a handball. I've lost in two FA Cup finals by an own goal but they pale compared to Anderlecht in terms of hurt.'

Two years later, Hodge would be involved in another major footballing controversy. It was his pass from which Diego Maradona capitalised and punched the ball into the England net. A deliberate back-pass? 'It was,' he says. 'I hit it with my strong left foot on the right side of the ball with the intention that it would spin back. It was a slice but it was an intended slice. I just thought that the goalkeeper would pick it up and we would squeeze up.'

Peter Shilton wasn't able to pick it up. Everyone in the stadium, everyone watching at home around the world, saw it was handball, apart from the one person that mattered – the referee, Ali Bin Nasser of Tunisia. Ending up with Maradona's shirt that day was little consolation but did later provide a neat title for Hodge's autobiography, *The Man with Maradona's Shirt*. How did that come about? 'I was walking down the tunnel and Maradona was coming in the opposite direction. I just tugged my shirt and we swapped there and then. I have no idea if he has still got mine.'

Let's hope so.

With the arrival of John Metgod, Hodge found his position under threat and left for Aston Villa and then on to Tottenham Hotspur before finding himself back at Forest for the start of the 1988/89 season. Neil Webb was now pulling the strings in the midfield so Hodge had a battle on to claim a shirt. In the opening game away at Norwich, Clough ensured Hodge knew he wouldn't stroll back into his reckoning for a place in the starting 11. At half-time, he gave Hodge a piece of advice, 'Harry darling. When you get the ball, give it to Neil Webb. He's a good midfield player.'

It was worth coming back though since he picked up two League Cup winners' medals. The first came after a 3-1 win against Luton Town in 1989, and a year later Forest successfully defended the trophy Clough had more than a dalliance with ten years previously by beating Oldham Athletic 1-0.

Against Luton, Forest made heavy weather of it and were a goal down at half-time. In the second half, having been told to speed up the passing, Forest roared back with the breakthrough being a well-taken Nigel Clough penalty after Hodge was felled in the area. First Webb then Clough again gave the scoreline a polished sheen. This trophy meant a lot to Brian and he would be grateful for Hodge's efforts that day.

Hodge recounts Brian's words to him, 'Harry darling. People don't forget. I don't forget that I was losing a League Cup Final 1-0, and you got my lad a penalty, you got my club a penalty, you got me and my club and my lad a penalty. He scored at Wembley because you got brought down at Wembley.'

As he hit his 30s, his calves started to tighten up and having spent a career hustling, bustling and scurrying around in midfield, Hodge wondered what was on the horizon for him. To compound his situation, a young Irishman by the name of Roy Keane was now tearing it up in the middle of the park. What's more, Clough loved Keane. Despite carrying an injury, Clough selected him ahead of Hodge for the 1991 FA Cup Final defeat to Tottenham Hotspur. Once more, Hodge's time at the City Ground was up.

He didn't curl up and metaphorically die under a stone though. He went to Leeds United and promptly won the final First Division title before the Premier League lumbered into view like a marauding monster.

Thinking back on what Brian said to him about remembering Hodge's contribution in wrestling the League Cup away from Luton's grip, he observes, 'That's what he was like – he'd remember little things like that ten years later.'

Steve Hodge will be remembered for his crucial goal at Celtic Park, his two headers against that team from Belgium and so much more besides for a good while yet.

John Metgod vs Manchester United (1984)

T HE 1984/85 season was not a great one for English football. Come the dénouement, death and violence would cloud the landscape. On the final day – 11 May – 56 lives were claimed and more than 200 people were injured at Bradford City's Valley Parade in a fire. Tragedy would also strike at Birmingham City where rioting held up play and later caused the collapse of a brick wall, killing a 14-year-old boy. Eighteen days later – 29 May – 39 spectators, most of them Italian, were killed when a wall collapsed at the European Cup Final between Liverpool and Juventus in Brussels at the woefully underprepared Heysel Stadium. Despite the tragedy, the match went ahead and Juventus were crowned European champions owing to a penalty converted by Michel Platini.

Football and goals are meaningless trivialities when set against such a context. Yet it is the hope for small moments of unconfined joy that drags people to football matches in the first instance. John Metgod provided not only one but two such 'pinch yourself' moments for Nottingham Forest fans.

Metgod was signed from Real Madrid in 1984 after 49 appearances. He had previously made his name for AZ Alkmaar, making 195 appearances and scoring 26 goals. Yet before AZ, it all started in Haarlem in north-west Netherlands. In his early teens, Metgod played for a select regional team and attracted the attention of various scouts.

He recalled, 'When I was 16, Barry Hughes, the Welshman who lived and worked for a long time in Holland, was at that time the manager of the first team at Haarlem. One day, he knocked on the door of my home and asked me to sign for them, which I did.'

The now defunct HFC Haarlem excelled in sourcing and developing talented players before selling them – Ruud Gullit being one prime example. Things moved fast for Metgod, 'I went in to the uder-18 team and they were more national than local or regional so you were travelling further for games. Then in December time of that first season, I moved up to the under-21s and scored.

'Then in my second season, I started in the first team squad. They were then in the Second Division and then I near enough played all the games. We won promotion to the First Division but I then went to AZ Alkmaar. I was there for six years; we won the Dutch league and the cup – three times I think – and we also played in the UEFA Cup Final against Ipswich, which we lost over two legs.'

That Ipswich Town team were no mugs and boasted players such as John Wark, Paul Mariner and Frans Thijssen – all of whom troubled the scoresheet over the two legs. Then in 1982, Metgod joined Real Madrid and played with José Antonio Camacho, Vicente del Bosque and Juanito.

During his two years in Madrid, *Los Merengues* somehow contrived to lose five finals in 1983: runners-up in La Liga, the European Cup Winners' Cup, the Copa del Rey, the Supercopa de España and the Copa de la Liga. Just for good measure, the league title was lost to Athletic Bilbao on the final day of the season. 'It's a piece of history – but not one you like to be remembered for!'

Opportunities were limited at Madrid though, and Metgod remembers, 'I had two years at Real Madrid but in those days you could only have two foreigners. They signed [Jorge] Valdano.

They already had [Ulrich] Stielike so I was the third one and I wasn't going to play unless there were injuries and I really wanted to play football so I went to Nottingham Forest. They already wanted to sign me when I signed for Real Madrid so I had already had a conversation with them.'

His debut for Forest came on the opening day of the 1984/85 season, at Sheffield Wednesday in a 3-1 loss where he found himself on the receiving end of a crunching tackle. Welcome to England. He says, 'The worst was the way they played. I played in midfield. I obviously wanted to get on the ball but [looks up into the sky, back and forth]. Wednesday had just got promoted so they were on a high and Lee Chapman was there – the ball was up in the air; it was horrendous.'

Sometimes deployed as a holding midfielder and on other times at centre-back, he looked as much at home in possession of the football as he looked uncomfortable when being asked to chase around and make reducer tackles. 'I remember a couple of times when I played in midfield and he [Brian Clough] said, "Can't you get a foot in and challenge and win the ball?" I said, "Gaffer, if you wanted me to do that, you should have signed somebody else because that's not my way of playing and I'm not the kind of guy to win tackles – that's not me."'

Not him indeed. Metgod's game was based around technique, passing and free kicks. Especially free kicks. It was on a freezing late afternoon in the dying days of 1984 that Metgod carved his mark into Forest folklore.

Ron Atkinson's Manchester United strolled into town with a very decent team featuring Paul McGrath, Bryan Robson and Arnold Muhren. They would bring home the FA Cup come the end of the season thanks to a Norman Whiteside goal in extra time to claim a 1-0 victory over that season's champions, Everton, at Wembley. Their tough-tackling defender Kevin Moran would become the first player to be sent off in an FA Cup Final when he would topple Peter Reid. Eighteen days later, a young man called Nigel would pull on the number nine shirt and make his debut for Forest in a 2-1 home win over Ipswich Town and Forest would stumble into ninth position in the final reckoning.

But that's all in the future. That's not important right now.

In the first half, United took the lead. Frank Stapleton beautifully dissected the Forest defence to send Alan Brazil through on goal. For some weird reason, Hans Segers decided to eschew the tried and trusted convention of utilising the flappy things on the end of his arms and slid in feet first with the glee and recklessness of an eight-year-old hurtling down a back-garden water slide on a summer's day. The result was inevitable – a penalty was awarded after Brazil ended up eating turf, limbs flailing like an upturned turtle.

Gordon Strachan dispatched the spot-kick with nonchalance, even taking the time to point to the corner of the goal in which the ball was snugly nestled as part of his celebration, as if to indicate that the resting place of the ball from this penalty was always thus.

Shortly after, a misplaced ball from the right-back area was intercepted in midfield and landed at the feet of Strachan. Although 25 yards out, he took aim for that very same bottom corner of the net and expertly found his target – not with pace or power but beautiful precision. Segers looked a defeated man, hunched shoulders and a wee midfielder pulling the same card trick on him.

Nonetheless, the stage was thus set for perhaps the most satisfying scoreline a fan can hope to enjoy. Steve Hodge reduced the arrears after finding himself one on one thanks in part to a deflection. With the minimum of fuss, he slammed the ball into the Trent End net.

In the 77th minute a trickle of a cross was woefully dealt with by the United defence. The ball fell to Gary Mills around nine yards out and he walloped it past Gary Bailey.

During the build-up, the distinctive gait of the rather avuncular figure of Metgod had lurked around the six-yard line after lumbering up to support the attack. He fancied a goal.

A comeback from two down, rescued in the last minute, was great – but it got better.

⚽ ⚽ ⚽

Forest are awarded a free kick deep into added time. The ball is positioned just outside the penalty area and Metgod steps up.

Ian Bowyer stands a few yards back, hands on hips – he's seen it all before; he was here when Brian Clough walked through the doors, he's scored a decisive goal in the European Cup semi-final, he's won the goddamn European Cup.

Having said that, he's probably seen free kicks ballooned over the bar more times than mere mortals like us have put socks on inside out.

But not this time.

Metgod ambles up to the ball and seems to scoop it over the wall with a side-foot. This is all before David Beckham's weird off-balance striking position and before Cristiano Ronaldo mastered the skill of making the ball go all wobbly at pace.

His strike is not powerful but it is perfectly placed in the top corner, beyond Bailey's despairing dive. He crumples to the floor with a thud just as the crowd behind him jump in unison. The fall of their first jump neatly coincides with Bailey's body clunking on to the damp, cold City Ground turf.

Technically speaking, it's a perfect kick.

⚽ ⚽ ⚽

Metgod remembers, 'It was pretty close to the edge of the box. The main thing about it, watching it now, is from that position, it's nearly impossible to get the right weight behind the ball because the distance is not enough – you've got to hit it technically perfectly because if you don't do that then it's too soft and the goalkeeper saves it or it's too hard and it doesn't come down enough and it goes over or hits the bar. So technically, it was a difficult one. It's more like a sort of chip with a bit of pace rather than a normal free kick.'

It's not only the winning free kick from that game that is seared into Metgod's memory, 'The one thing that sticks out from that game is – I think if you analysed my performance in that game – it would be...pretty bad. It was surely not one of my best games – not one to remember!'

There are numerous factors which make this goal particularly memorable: in a beautiful symmetry of tessellation, all of the goals are at the same end; the kit sported is a club classic, the SKOL sponsor; the cold, dark early evening of a winter's game at the final whistle after the sepia sunlight of the early afternoon kick-off; the celebration...oh my, the celebration.

⚽⚽⚽

He runs towards the Brian Clough Stand (then the highfaluting Executive Stand) with all the athleticism of Carl Lewis...but only briefly. Suddenly the adrenaline starts to subside – he slows. The right arm is used to punch the air, mimicked neatly by Davenport in pursuit. A brief windmill with the same right arm and then...where is everyone? Keep up, fools. Where are you? What kept you?

He is eventually caught and halted, at which point, he looks absolutely done for, relieved that he can now stop.

⚽⚽⚽

'After having scored quite a number of free kicks, Ian Bowyer said, "We're not going to bother anymore to try and catch you up in the celebration because you seem to be able to generate more pace than in the game!"' Metgod recalls.

Such magical moments don't occur in a vacuum. Not everyone can step up and stick the ball in to the net with such frequency from dead ball situations. He says, 'You've got the ability within you as a result of your passing ability or your accuracy but surely it needs practising. I can't say that I practised every day after training sessions but I did practise.'

It's not just technical expertise that yields such bounty though – there's a long psychological game at play too. He explains, 'If you hit it one side but change it the next time, eventually the goalkeeper doesn't know where to go. You want to put doubt in the keeper's mind: sometimes you go over the wall, sometimes you go for the far corner, you bend it around the wall, but you vary it and by varying it, it puts doubt in the goalkeeper's mind because he doesn't know what I'm going to do. After I scored one or two free kicks, they were focused on trying to cater for both corners and stood centrally, meaning this opened up both corners for me to aim for.'

Many goalkeepers found themselves picking the ball out of the net after Metgod hovered over a dead ball around the edge of the penalty area. Sticking one past one of the greatest goalkeepers certainly helps cultivate that psychological edge he had in such situations.

'Of all the free kicks I took, probably the most important one, but for a different reason, was the one against Southampton at home where Peter Shilton was in goal. Before that, everybody said, "Well, yeah, he's all right, he can take a free kick and that" but then I scored one against Peter Shilton and it wasn't over the wall but it was bent into the far corner which was normally considered to be the goalkeeper's corner and I think general opinion after that was if you are able to score in that corner against a goalkeeper like Peter Shilton, then you must be pretty decent at taking free kicks.'

Of course, there is *that* other free kick goal, which came later against West Ham United on 2 April 1986: *that* goal for which he is most famous. *That* goal against West Ham and *that* accompanying celebration.

Scott Murray of *The Guardian* beautifully captured both events, 'The best goal of the 1980s, and the greatest celebration of them all as well. His side having been awarded a free kick at least 30 yards from goal, Forest midfielder Johnny Metgod – a taller, funkier, less desperate version of George Costanza – stepped up to take it. Subtlety was not in his mind: he simply belaboured the ball in a straight line, thinking (not unreasonably) that anyone getting in the way would either be taken with it, or decapitated.

'As it arrowed into the roof of title-chasing West Ham's net, Metgod simply turned round and prodded his finger in the air five times. An innocently gleeful act which communicated the sheer violence of the strike, in the style of a barstool philosopher who has slipped into "But this is what I'm saying" mode after his seventh pint.'

The best goal of the 1980s? Perhaps. The most startling goal of the 1980s? Definitely. The most iconic celebration of the 1980s? Undoubtedly. The main himself says, 'As soon as it left my foot, I knew it was a clean strike. I didn't know it was going to go in but I knew it was the cleanest of strikes that I ever hit. And you know that from the moment it leaves your foot. I hardly felt it so that means it's good contact.

'From that distance, you have to keep it low as usually your body goes up or backwards and the ball goes up. So the only thing I concentrated on with that one was to keep it low and hit the target – that's all you can do.'

But the winner against Manchester United in added time to herald a famous comeback, well...we're deep into the woods of football fan perfection with this goal.

The talented Dutchman would spend three years Trentside, making 116 appearances and scoring 15 goals, before being sold to Spurs where he lasted only a season.

'It didn't work out,' he recalls of his London experience. 'David Pleat signed me but he got sacked at the end of October and I picked up the only injury I ever had that needed surgery – a hernia.

'At the time I was recovering and Terry Venables came in early December and I was only ready to play again in mid-January. Glenn Hoddle left to play for Monaco and I came in and I was seen by the press as his replacement, which I wasn't. But that's the sort of stigma you get. To try and get away from that was impossible.'

It was then back to his homeland with Feyenoord before embarking upon an extensive coaching career in Holland, England (Portsmouth and Derby) and America (Colorado

Rapids) before eventually returning to the banks of the Trent as a director.

Metgod reminisces upon his playing stint in Nottingham with deep fondness, 'I really, really enjoyed it – not only the football but also the life. We lived in West Bridgford and my son went to school here. My daughter was born here. She was made in Spain but born in Nottingham! My time in Nottingham has always been really enjoyable. We still stay in touch with friends and neighbours from when we first moved here. We are firm believers that whatever experience you have in whatever country you are in, it's all about you but not you as an individual but you as a family to try and make the most of it.'

Like all who flourished under Brian Clough, he recalls how his boss reduced the often over-complicated game to a simple one. 'It was very very simple: everybody knew what they had to do in their positions. Cloughie wasn't one to complicate things: he kept it very basic – do whatever you are good at.'

John Metgod possessed a right foot capable of unleashing symbiotic power and beauty. His goals are an important brick in the history of Nottingham Forest.

Nigel Clough vs Manchester United (1986)

TOWERING far-post headers. Scuffed shots from six yards out that trickle over the line. Shots rifled in from the edge of the box with laser-like precision. Overhead kicks that risk a good old shoeing to the head. Penalties blasted in to the corner – top, bottom, either – it's all the same to him.

Twenty-five yard free kicks that sail serenely past the goalkeeper's despairing outstretched right hand. Impudent back-heels from the near post. Delightfully lofted chips over the keeper from the edge of the area. Razor-sharp turns with his back to goal with a defender's close and intimate attention before firing in. Powering runs right through the heart of a defence.

Nigel Clough scored all types of goals – and lots of them.

He remains Nottingham Forest's second-highest scorer with 131 goals from 311 games (discounting his spell as a returning loanee). Clough is sandwiched between Grenville Morris and Wally Ardron, with Johnny Dent and Ian Storey-Moore following behind, providing a clear indication that for all the love and adulation afforded to strikers like Stan Collymore, Nigel is often overlooked as a Forest hero.

For five out of six seasons, the name Clough topped the Forest goalscoring charts between 1985 and 1991. Just in case you were wondering, it was Steve Hodge who interrupted his reign in 1989/90 – with Nigel coming in a close second.

The fact that Nigel was also a huge Forest fan since 1975 is often overlooked too. He grew up watching his heroes Garry Birtles, John Robertson and Ian Bowyer conquering Europe from the stands (and occasionally the bench) and remembers fondly the evening in Köln when a first European final was secured.

Forget the identity of his father and take a moment to see Nigel Clough as a fan, a special player and a heck of a goalscorer in Nottingham Forest's history.

As a player, he often seemed like he was wallowing in treacle while struggling to remove the great bloody big deep-sea diving boots someone had stuck on his feet for a jape. His legs frequently looked like they would buckle under the weight of a bag of sugar. When striking a ball towards goal, he often slid to the ground in order to apply just that little more power – or maybe simply because he was out of breath having used all his energy to get to the ball in the first place.

Yet when you are effective at both creating space for midfielders, wingers and a marauding left-back to exploit as well as banging in goals in nearly every third game you play, none of the apparent weaknesses in your game matter.

Watch a show reel of his goals and often he is out of shot while the play is going on around him. This is due to him having frequently dropped deep towards the start of the move and while Stuart Pearce or Gary Crosby or Franz Carr or Neil Webb are bearing down on goal, Nigel is making his way to the penalty area in his own sweet time, invariably popping up to apply the finishing touch to the move he started. He was not only a creator but also a poacher with a striker's instinct.

His boss knew he had a player on his hands and what's more, he knew a decent striker when he clapped eyes on one. 'I constructed the team around him to get the best out of him and it worked, not only for the team but for individuals within it,' explained Clough senior in his autobiography.

'For instance, Stuart Pearce said to me on one of those occasions when he was accusing me of being too hard on the lad, "I wouldn't be half the player I am without your Nige in the side – and I play left-back." Even Teddy Sheringham, with whom I didn't get on that well, told me after the one full season of his, "I've scored 20-odd goals this year but without your Nige in the side I wouldn't have got ten." Oh yes, the players knew he had talent.'

Graham Taylor tells of how he felt the key to stopping Forest was to isolate Nigel. In Paul McGrath's book, *Back from the Brink*, he recalls, 'I remember we played Nottingham Forest. They played good stuff, but were defensive to a degree where they'd let you come on to them and try to hit you on the break.

'It took me a while to work it out. They played Nigel Clough outside-right and this day, I used Paul [McGrath] to man-mark him. To me, a lot of Forest's football came through Clough. Great player, but he couldn't run.

'So I told Paul to follow Clough wherever he went. They were moving him all over the place to try and bring him into the game. Paul would look across at me. "Follow him," I kept saying. Anyway, we won 2-1. Cloughie never got a kick.

'Couldn't figure it out afterwards why it had taken me about five years to work them out...'

In many ways, this anecdote reveals more about Clough as a player than McGrath as a defender. Forget nepotism, Nigel got in the side because he was good enough – easily good enough – more than good enough. After all, his father proudly declared, 'Our Nige was a bloody good player who could pass a ball as well as anybody and who scored more than his fair share of goals.'

A bright lad, Nigel was strongly encouraged to stay on and do A Levels when he was a kid. The problem was that he kept scoring goals for Heanor Town. His footballing talent couldn't go on being ignored, underused and overlooked. So he went and played for Forest reserves and kept scoring goals. Eventually, it was time to give him a shot in the first team.

'*Pass the gravy, son, and by the way, get yourself up those apples and pears early tonight as you're playing in my first team tomorrow.*'

Sadly, these words were never spoken around the Clough family dinner table on Christmas Day of 1984. It would, however, be the day after that, on a cold Boxing Day at the City Ground, that the name Clough first appeared on a Nottingham Forest team sheet. Typical of Brian, the young debutant knew nothing about this until the day of the game. Not a hint was offered the previous day in the Clough household over crackers, turkey and Christmas dinner.

Nigel took the place of struggling striker Trevor Christie, who was a very good egg about seeing his place taken by his boss's son and wished him good luck. Of course, when your boss is Brian Clough, it's probably wise to be magnanimous in such an awkward situation.

The choice of day was poignant for Nigel's dad. 'It was Boxing Day 1984 – exactly 22 years from the very day when I crumpled under that goalkeeper's challenge at Roker Park, to be carried off on a stretcher, my playing career effectively over,' he said.

Like Hodge before him, Nigel was up against a formidable Ipswich Town team featuring Terry Butcher in defence.

Picking a raw 18-year-old to make his debut against one of the division's most feared defenders is like asking the work experience lad to stand in the Commons and face Prime Minister's Questions from a baying opposition, but as usual, Brian knew what he was doing. It was character-building and would stand his young striker in good stead for the years to come – assuming he made it off the pitch in one piece, that is.

Nigel did indeed come through this traumatic experience and went on to make nine more appearances and bag a goal in his debut season. In truth, he wasn't an instant success – that would come later. As it was though, he amazingly played non-contract in his first full season – an unthinkable situation now in the era of contracts thicker than the Argos Christmas catalogue.

He also managed to play Sunday league football for his brother's team – Hunters FC – on a park in Derby after turning out for his dad's team the day before. He had signed for them at the start of the season and was told to see out the contract by someone who held sway over such decisions in the Clough household. Nigel just got on with things in his own steady and dignified manner.

There was no special treatment for Nigel. Just like everyone else, he would spend pre-season training running around a lake in Wollaton Park in Nottingham for a week until the footballs came out the following week. Running never was Nigel's strength as a player so he eased the tedium and pain with the thoughts of revenge on the dreaded lake in the style of a comic book super villain. 'I used to dream, when I was running around it, of coming back and blowing it up so no one else had to run round it,' he said.

Later on in his managerial career, he would, in a very roundabout way, complete his revenge – but no Acme explosives were used. While at the helm at Derby County, he and his managerial team of John Metgod and Gary Crosby took their team for a run round the dreaded lake. They even had a little jog around it themselves – in all likelihood, a much slower jog.

For all his delicate touches and sweeping sashays, Nigel would have to show his mettle on the pitch – not to his team-mates, but to the opposition. This he did. 'He cracked it one day against Arsenal, Tony Adams in particular,' his father recounted. 'I grew angry at the sight of him crashing into Nigel from the back, time after time. So I called my lad to the touchline and said, "The first time you get the chance – cut Adams in half." Arsenal's manager, George Graham, leapt out of the other dug-out. "There's no need for that, Brian," he said.

'"Hey," I told George, "I've been watching him clatter our centre-forward for the past 20 f**king minutes and he hasn't faced him once yet. Everything's coming in from the back."

'Within minutes our Nige had turned with the ball, approached Adams face on – and gone straight through. Not over the ball but just powered right through the lad, leaving him on the deck wondering what the hell had hit him. Word went round. Nobody messed with him after that.'

Nigel was starting to carve his own name into the consciousness of top-flight football. He was a brave player too – not only brave in the sense of one of his dad's favourite traits, receiving the ball while under pressure, regardless of how well you are playing, but also brave in the sense of willing to do anything in order to put the round thing into the onion bag.

In Duncan Hamilton's book, *Provided You Don't Kiss Me: 20 Years with Brian Clough*, there is a photograph of Nigel scoring a goal at the City Ground. Underneath the picture is this caption: 'Nigel Clough planting a diving header into the net. It was this picture about which his father took great pride, pointing out his son's wide-open eyes and boasting about his bravery and awareness.'

Young Clough was a key figure in the Nottingham Forest team that spent the mid-to-late-80s knocking the ball around on the deck and avoiding the referee's wrath, while also claiming some serious silverware.

It was Nigel who scored twice against Luton Town in the 1989 League Cup Final and bagged a man of the match award to claim Forest's first major trophy in nine years – their first since the 1980 European Cup.

While the media seemed fixated on the notion of the win meaning a lot to his father, Nigel beautifully and deftly deflected Martin Tyler's line of questioning in his post-match interview which probed this line of enquiry, 'I know what it means to me and that team and those supporters.'

A year later, Nigel once again played a key role in successfully retaining the League Cup by playing Nigel Jemson clean through for a one on one against Oldham Athletic's Andy Rhodes which he dispatched at the second time of asking.

In typical Brian fashion, there were few celebrations on the bus home. In fact, as they disembarked on their return to Nottingham – gleaming League Cup trophy with red and white ribbons safely in their possession – the players were asked to report for training the next day for some running since in truth, they had won the final without playing very well at all.

Regrets? Like his old man's favourite singer, he has a few. It is the FA Cup Final defeat to Tottenham Hotspur that rankles with Nigel. Of course, he wanted to win it for himself, for the club, for the fans but also in this instance, for his old man. He wistfully admits that it wasn't their day yet still finds it difficult to accept some of referee Roger Milford's 'incredible decisions' on that day after failing to even book Paul Gascoigne for leaving a six-stud indentation on Garry Parker's chest and attempting to remove the lower leg of Gary Charles. It is the sight of Milford smiling with Gascoigne and patting him on the back as he was being stretchered off that haunts him.

Like every young boy coming to terms with the adult world around him, there is a defining moment – a moment which dares the boy to believe that he does indeed belong in the crazy mixed-up world in which he find himself shambling around. Perhaps Nigel's epiphany came at Old Trafford on a muddy pitch in January of 1986 in front of a crowd of 46,717.

Forest were 2-1 down in the 82nd minute until Colin Walsh burst through on goal and smashed a low shot past Gary Bailey, which nestled in the net after bouncing agonisingly off the foot of both posts. A more aesthetically pleasing goal you couldn't wish to see.

⚽ ⚽ ⚽

But the drama isn't over; it is just getting started.

Deep in the throes of injury time, Walsh plays a short corner to Neil Webb who swivels to afford himself half a yard and then dinks the ball to the back post where Nigel nods in to secure a famous win.

Arms, legs, dentures everywhere.

⚽ ⚽ ⚽

Nigel Clough was no longer a novelty, an interesting topic of conversation, a father's son. He was a match-winning scorer on one of the biggest stages in the top division. Wearing a mud-splattered all-yellow away kit, the win rekindled memories of the famous 4-0 trouncing dished out to United at Old Trafford on Forest's way to the title in the 1977/78 season. At the sight of Nigel's header hitting the net, Brian ambles up the camber of the Old Trafford turf and does a little jig. Nigel celebrates in his usual fashion: one arm (two arms aloft for a particularly significant goal) followed by a good old-fashioned proper handshake for whoever assisted him.

It wasn't easy for Nigel to be there when the end of his father's management career eventually came. He describes the weeks leading up to confirmation of this as his worst time in football. He had to be a supportive son as well as a player toiling in a troubled and desperate team. He spent nine years supporting the club from the sidelines and a further nine years as a player. All the while, he had a front-row seat to his father's ailing health and powers.

Relegation seemed like the end of an era, to him more than anyone else, so with his contract up he left for Liverpool. This wasn't out of desperation to better himself or collect medals or to protect his international prospects or from preciousness of dropping down a league. It was simply that he felt, certainly from the point of view of the club, that a break with the Clough name might well be best for all concerned. His love for Nottingham Forest ran deep – deeper than many realise. Young Clough – 'the number nine' to his father – had always faced the problem of being accepted as a player in his own right so once he decided to take the step into management, he was used to the comparisons.

In his green days as a player, he gained acceptance from his boyhood idols in the shape of John Robertson, Garry Birtles and Ian Bowyer and having achieved this, he encountered few problems. In fact, it was just as difficult for his father as it was for him to go the extra mile to avoid charges of nepotism.

Brian once suggested it might be easier for his son to look elsewhere but Nigel was having none of it: he was a supporter since 1975 and there was nowhere else he wanted to play. He simply adopted the best strategy there was to gaining acceptance: score goals. Do your job. Be good enough. Don't be a tittle-tattle.

Nigel knew from the start this would have to be a rule he would adhere to as closely as the first rule of *Fight Club*. His father pinpointed the exact moment his son was no longer the gaffer's lad but one of the boys. 'I knew Nigel had been accepted the day we were travelling back on the coach from somewhere and I happened to overhear Des Walker,' Brian recalled. 'We were giving a lift to one of his mates, whom I saw tap Des on the shoulder, point towards Clough junior and then put a finger to his lips. Walker immediately turned on him and said in a low voice, "Don't you ever doubt him. He's dead straight. You could tell anything and it will stick."'

By his own admission, Brian was tough on his son at work. 'I treated him far worse than I treated the other players,' but the pride glows through his father's words regarding his son. 'I do believe [he] deserves the utmost credit, not only for the way he endured me as his boss, but for the dignified manner in which he has conducted himself.'

Not only a successful goalscorer, young Clough proved himself to be a very adept manager in guiding Burton Albion from non-league football to the brink of promotion to League 2 in 2009, then he returned in 2015 and took them up from League 1 to the Championship.

Maybe his father reserves special pride for this achievement as he knew just how hard and lonely management could be. 'I know he was proud [having picked up the UniBond League championship trophy which meant promotion to the now National League] but he couldn't have felt prouder than his old man even though we had won other cups together with me as the gaffer and him in the team,' said Brian.

It was Nigel Clough who scored the final goal of the season that brought the curtain down on his career as the club around which he grew up from smiling boy to man in a defeat in the final game of 1992/93. This goal at Portman Road was also the last of his father's time at Forest and in football management.

It seems apt that Nigel made his debut against Ipswich: the club against whom Frank Clark scored his single solitary goal at their Portman Road home. The scene for Steve Hodge's Forest debut. The place where the curtain came down on Nigel's stellar Forest career and at the same time, his old man's interstellar management career.

Football is weird like that sometimes – throwing up little coincidences and patterns. Although Nigel's story will always be inextricably intertwined with his father's, he made not just the old man proud but also a generation of Nottingham Forest fans proud.

Brian Rice vs Arsenal (1988)

EACH and every club has a player that is held in higher regard than perhaps he deserves to be. The reasons for such status vary greatly: bucketloads of effort to compensate for a lack of talent perhaps or a fleeting period of unsustainable genius maybe. In Brian Rice's case, his elevation to sanctity can be attributed to a few seconds in north London on a freezing Saturday afternoon in March 1988.

Beyond the borders of Nottingham, Brian Rice is a name that slipped through the wider football consciousness, through the wide cracks in the pavement to be picked up once in a while out of nostalgic interest but then quickly discarded.

Between 1985 and 1991, Rice made 92 appearances for Brian Clough's second great Forest team, which seemingly camped out at Wembley to contest various finals while also managing to trouble third place in the First Division table in successive seasons. Greatness? Compared to successive European Cup victories and the odd league title, this team falls short but two League Cups equals those brought home by Clough and Peter Taylor in their heyday.

This late-80s team was manufactured in the midst of a post-party comedown for Nottingham Forest, which was still playing off the debts for the construction of the Executive Stand (now the Brian Clough Stand). Clough himself was flying solo after his acrimonious fall-out with his old mate Peter Taylor and labouring under the self-imposed pressure to prove he could do it all again on his own and that he hadn't 'shot it' – to use a Taylorism. Under such terms and conditions, this was indeed a great Nottingham Forest team.

Rice was not a central cog in this team. He frittered up and down the left wing and his running style was more mechanical than fluent. He lacked pace, was hesitant in front of goal and delivered wayward crosses. John Robertson, he wasn't.

But in many ways, he was the epitome of a Clough footballer: brave, always available for the ball and neat and tidy in possession. His striking red hair and upright gait ensured he stood out from the crowd. As Duncan Hamilton recalls in *Provided You Don't Kiss Me: 20 Years with Brian Clough*, Clough said of Rice, 'I'm not saying he's thin and pale, but the maid in our hotel remade his bed without realising he was still in it.'

To this day, songs are sung about Brian and t-shirts declaring his name are proudly worn. Like most things, the reasons for such reverence are not always simple and straightforward – more often than not, such status is bestowed due to a combination of factors but Rice's goal makes up the lion's share of reasons why he is still so beloved.

The team Rice played in was one that went under the radar for the rest of the footballing world. Speaking to Nottingham Forest periodical *Bandy and Shinty*, the Scot is quick to praise Brian Clough for instilling the correct footballing virtues into the team. 'That all came from the gaffer,' Rice recalls. 'Everything had to be played forward and we had fantastic pace in the team with wee Franz Carr. We had Garry Birtles, we had Steve Hodge making his runs and Pearcey bombing up that line. I don't think I can ever remember us having to sit in and defend, when we got it we just attacked. There was no fear. With Franz on the wing and Des at the back, we could catch a greyhound.

'Not a lot of people talk about this but these were fantastic individual players: Johnny Metgod, Stuart Pearce, Steve Hodge, Neil Webb, young Nigel but every one of these lads recognised that the team was more important than the individual. All of these international players and I was just a wee nobody from Scotland.'

Famously, the FA Cup eluded Clough's outstretched hands, which had previously grasped every other pot and trinket. The

1987/88 season was going well though and 15 wins from 26 league games (and only five defeats) kept his side in contention for third place – where they would ultimately finish – when the quarter-final rumbled around. Forest had not enjoyed a home draw in the cup thus far and a trip to Highbury represented a significant obstacle on the road to Wembley. The third round saw a tricky sojourn to The Shay but Halifax Town were easily disposed of in a 4-0 win. Next up, Forest faced former European Cup winner Frank Clark's Leyton Orient and squeezed through 2-1 thanks to two late goals from Lee Glover and Calvin Plummer.

Birmingham City were next to be vanquished – a solitary goal from the waif-like Gary Crosby was the difference after a beautiful pass from Nigel Clough set him free. Such progress in this competition was unusual for Forest, Clough and the supporters. That tangible feeling of it being their year lingered around the banks of the Trent.

At Highbury, Paul Wilkinson hammered Forest into the lead in the first half after a neat interchange with young Nigel. His rasping shot from 25 yards out left John Lukic rolling around like a playful puppy. Forest were playing well with the number nine causing all manner of problems for an intimidating back four comprising of Kenny Sansom, Tony Adams, David O'Leary and Nigel Winterburn. All the while, his father looked on impassively from the greenhouse-like Highbury dugout, no doubt concealing his pride.

Forest's ascendency continued into the second half. Somehow neither Crosby nor Wilkinson managed to double the lead after Crosby was put through one-on-one. An excellent recovery by Winterburn thwarted Crosby and Wilkinson screwed the rebound just wide. The famous Arsenal back four were on the ropes by now, encapsulated by Adams standing with his arm in the air appealing for offside as Crosby scampered through. This young and energetic Forest side was undoing the high line that he was marshalling.

Moments later, with the Arsenal defence pushed up to the halfway line, Rice's legendary status was crafted.

Clough tenaciously wins the ball in midfield and lobs it to his mate Crosby wide right. The ball spoons backwards – Crosby is facing his own goal with the experienced Sansom breathing down his neck. No matter. He spins inside and rather than running upfield to await a through ball, Clough goes to help him out. Crosby pings the ball to Clough's feet.

Paul Davis closes him down but Clough adjusts his feet with the grace of Darcy Bussell in order to buy himself some time, look up and leave Davis briefly grasping the floor. Meanwhile, Rice has meandered to the halfway line in acres of space. He knows Clough will somehow extricate himself from the Arsenal pincer – all he has to do is run – stay onside – but run. This he does.

A strange sound floats over the area. It is partly a collective appreciative mumble directed towards the Forest number nine. If distilled into one voice, it would probably translate to something like 'good ball'. Mixed into this is a collective groan from the Highbury faithful – there is only a chasm where a burly defender should be. It's the sound of panic and fear.

After this comes silence – a long, deafening and seemingly eternal silence. Rice is clean through – he's not quick but nobody is going to catch him: Clough's exquisite through ball ensures this to be so. Rice takes the ball in his stride, dinking it on to the pure, green space ahead of him. He is Dorothy skipping through the field towards Emerald City.

The problem with Emerald City though is that it was a sham, a charlatan, and one big dream-killing illusion. The Forest fans sense the futility of it all. They've just watched Crosby spurn a similar chance. It should be Clough or Wilkinson bearing down on Lukic. But it isn't. It's Brian Rice. He doesn't know what to do. He's moving too slow. He's too square on – there's no angle. He hasn't got the pace to take it round Lukic and Lukic ain't moving. He stands, granite-like.

⚽ ⚽ ⚽

Rice was confident in his own ability to make this one count. He remembered, 'I'm going to tell you something, right? Do you know what my nickname is and has always been though football? Chipper. I've always been known as Chipper – everyone in Scotland, everyone knows me as Chipper. I always fancied myself to score in one on ones.

'The ball from Nigel made the goal – it was probably one of the best passes I've ever seen. He played it with just the right amount of pace and all it needed was a good touch and I was through. I know and probably my team-mates know and are confident that I'm going to score. I was certain I was going to score, absolutely certain.

'I'd done it every day in training and was confident in my ability to do it. In such a situation, it's a battle of wills – who is going to stay up the longest? Is the goalkeeper going to stay up or am I going to panic? But there was no way I was going to panic. Lukic made the move and then it was my turn to move. I was in total control of the situation.'

⚽ ⚽ ⚽

Indeed he is. After what seems like an aeon of a staring contest between these two momentary adversaries, Rice adjusts his step. His feet re-organise themselves so as to free up his left foot in order to shoot. Lukic stays upright as long as he can but he senses Rice will blast it along the floor, perhaps close to his body. After all, Lukic has done his homework assiduously: there's only a very acute angle available to Rice – in order to score, he's going to have to opt for power.

But Rice has the upper hand. He ever so delicately scoops the ball upwards. Lukic arches backwards, as if a puppet master pulls the string firmly downwards. He is gazing up at the battleship grey sky and sees only a ball, gently arcing its way casually over him before bouncing gracefully into the unguarded net. A legend is born.

❂ ❂ ❂

On his trudge back to his own half to await Arsenal kicking off, Rice briefly chuckled to himself. Maybe he was revelling in the impetuousness of his dinked finish. Maybe it was relief. Maybe he could see a future ahead at Forest – perhaps lifting the FA Cup. No matter: it reminds us all that football is fun, a game to be played with your mates, which can occasionally produce such moments of bliss.

Clough briefly stepped out of and then back into his dugout – he looked nervous. He was nervous. He later told Duncan Hamilton, 'I want to win the FA Cup very badly – but don't say that unless we do win it.' Before the 1991 cup final defeat to Tottenham Hotspur, at the precise time of that Rice goal, he was arguably the closest he had ever been to doing so.

John Motson acknowledged the build-up to the goal in his commentary, 'His son Nigel made the goal that may have killed off George Graham's team. One of the best pieces of appreciation of the game you'll see this season. Many players would have pushed the ball the other way but Clough was so aware.'

When Brian talked endlessly about brave players who want the ball and don't hide, his son's shimmy to take the harder option and turn to face the congested midfield rather than bang it back to Crosby down the wing is perhaps the clearest example of what he meant by this.

Forest lost out at Hillsborough in the semi-final to Liverpool, who themselves went on to be defeated by Wimbledon at Wembley. Brian Clough never did get his hands on the FA Cup.

Brian Rice found a place in the hearts of Forest fans and remains there to this day. After a few loan spells away from the City Ground, he moved back to Scotland in 1991 to join Falkirk. He drifted around in Scottish football, going on to represent

Dunfermline Athletic, Clyde and, just the once, Greenock Morton in 2000.

He would later surface in Qatar as a coach for Al-Khor Sporting Club but things turned sour in 2013 when reports surfaced of him being held in a Qatari jail as a result of gambling debts, drawing concern in Nottingham. Fortunately, he resurfaced alive and well to become a close confidant of John Hughes, and together they enjoyed success with Inverness Caledonian Thistle.

Rice's song occasionally still gets an airing when either Forest are cruising to victory or, more often than not, trying to dull the pain of an away defeat. It takes supporters back to the good old days of the late 1980s, to Highbury and to the time when Brian Rice produced a beautiful and everlasting moment.

Number 1 is Brian Rice.
Number 2 is Brian Rice.
Number 3 is Brian Rice.
Number 4 is Brian Rice.
Number 5 is Brian Rice.
Number 6 is Brian Rice.
Number 7 is Brian Rice.
Number 8 is Brian Rice.
Number 9 is Brian Rice.
Number 10 is Brian Rice.
Number 11 is Brian Rice.
Number 12 is Brian Rice.
We all live in a world of Brian Rice.
A world of Brian Rice.
A world of Brian Rice.

Garry Parker vs Everton (1989)

THE Full Members' Cup came into being as a result of the ban imposed on English clubs from competing in European competitions after the Heysel Stadium disaster in 1985.

In the absence of the European Cup, UEFA Cup and the sadly defunct European Cup Winners' Cup, this gave clubs a shot at competing for another trophy alongside the FA Cup, League Cup and the championship.

It ran from 1986 to 1992, enjoying various sponsors along the way including Simod and the enjoyably futuristic Zenith Data Systems. Ignored by some, mocked by others, it nonetheless produced some highly enjoyable and surprisingly open finals with bags of goals and scorelines resembling tennis sets. But it was all hugely enjoyable for those who cared to throw their boots into the ring.

Nottingham Forest loved a day out at Wembley around this time. If there was a trophy available, Brian Clough would send his team out to win it and Garry Parker was a vital cog in the club's residency at the famous old stadium.

Signed from Hull City for £250,00 in 1988 after a frustrating start to his career at Luton Town under David Pleat, Parker slotted neatly into Forest's intricate triangles forged between Nigel Clough, Neil Webb, Stuart Pearce and Gary Crosby. Dubbed Mr Suntan by the legendary *Brian* fanzine at the time, he looked right at home in the 80s with the occasional streaked highlight to add to his seemingly permatan. But boy, this lad could play football and instead of a foot on the end of his right leg, he just happened to have a beautifully ripe peach.

Having already claimed the League Cup earlier in April and seeming destined to achieve a highly commendable third place in the First Division, Forest came into this game full of confidence against a strong but ultimately disappointing Everton team who would complete the season in eighth. However, if Clough's men were to bring home another trophy, they were going to do it the hard way.

Things didn't go swimmingly from the start. Tony Cottee's run dissected the centre of the Forest defence like a cheese wire through bubbles and handed the Toffeemen the initiative.

No matter though, as a Tommy Gaynor corner bundled its way across the edge of the Everton six-yard line towards Parker who volleyed the ball into the ground and somehow found a gap between the defender stationed inertly on the line and the post. Neville Southall wearily clambered to his feet and turned as if to ask how on God's good earth has that one squeezed into the net. A tidy goal for Parker but that's not the one that lasts long in the memory, and after a level first half the party was only just getting started.

Kevin Sheedy maintained the high standards with a searching ball from the halfway line having spotted Graeme Sharp plodding towards the Forest goal. With Terry Wilson and Des Walker bearing down on him, he knew he wouldn't get much closer to the goal and so understandably smacked one in despite being 25 yards out. It was a beautiful finish to take Everton back into the lead.

⚽ ⚽ ⚽

And then it happens. Part of what makes Parker's goal so celebrated and memorable is the fact that it all stems from an Everton corner, swung in by Pat Nevin. This puts the Forest defence in a bit of a tizzle – Wilson attempts to head the ball clear at the front post but makes a bit of a hash of it and only succeeds in flicking it backwards across the six-yard line. Cottee is lurking but all he can do is crumple to the floor and the ball finds its way to the safe feet of Des Walker. It's all okay – Des has got it. Wait. What's he doing? He's dribbling the ball a mere four yards from his own goal. Whack it, Des. Get rid of it, Des.

But Des knows better. He's Des Walker.

He progresses beyond the penalty spot, has a quick look up and shapes to clear it with his left foot. It is clearly apparent that this isn't just a hoof it clearance – he's seen his mate, the young number nine – our Nigel – making himself available as an outlet betwixt and between the centre circle and his own penalty area.

Our Nigel has now grown accustomed to being clattered from behind by some burly bruiser so he ever so sweetly and deftly strokes the ball to the forward-running Parker with one delightful touch. Parker is clear but he's still deep in his own half and the only support he's got is our Nigel who, bless him, isn't blessed with pace.

The wide-open green space of Wembley lies before him. He runs forward with the ball – Kevin Ratcliffe isn't getting any closer to him. He shifts the direction of his run slightly towards the right side – he knows he's got to create an angle for the shot before he gets caught since he too knows that in shuttle sprints in training, he and the number nine would saunter in last.

Incredibly, he makes it to the edge of the Everton penalty area. He shapes to shoot but hesitates for a split second – the angle's not quite right, his shape could use some amendment. He allows the ball to run a yard further. Now. Perfect.

Southall is on the six-yard line – there's not much to aim at. He could blast it – after all, he must be shattered having run from what might as well be the coach car park outside the stadium. But no, he trusts his right foot and backs himself. The ball is slotted neatly into Southall's bottom-right corner. He's only gone and scored one of the great Wembley goals.

Given this, he's rather casual as he trots on a few more yards – obligatory inflatables wave jauntily in the away end. Gaynor,

Lee Chapman and our Nigel catch up with him and give him a big hug. He's earned it. Extra time beckons.

Apart from the whole move stemming from virtually the Forest goal line, it's the calmness that makes the goal special.

⚽ ⚽ ⚽

Parker had a knack for scoring special goals on special occasions, none more so than the thunderbolt he smacked in at Ashton Gate in the semi-final of the League Cup to eventually see off the almighty challenge of Bristol City in extra time under biblical rain. It was also Parker's goal at Old Trafford that secured Forest's passage to the semi-final of the FA Cup in 1989 after excellent work down the right from Franz Carr. Admittedly, this wasn't the FA Cup Final – it was the Full Members' Cup after all – but it was a Wembley final and the chance to slot another trophy in to the cabinet, an achievement that Clough would never underestimate. Sure enough, Forest went on to secure the trophy in extra time. Chapman chipped his team into the lead only for Cottee to bag his second with a header from a Pat Nevin cross. This extra time malarkey was pulsating stuff.

In the second period, Steve Sutton somehow prevented Sharp's effort crossing the line by deflecting his low shot up and on to the crossbar before getting up and running towards his own goal to catch the thing on its way down. It's a minor miracle that he prevented himself from carrying the ball over the line but he surely did since the only other person with a clear view of this is Cottee as he found himself in the back of the Forest goal. He clutched his head in frustration, clearly indicating to all and sundry that the ball hadn't crossed the line.

Fair play to him for his Corinthian values – no doubt a player in his boots these days would celebrate the goal regardless in an effort to convince the officials that the ball was over. It was clearly Forest's day.

For the umpteenth time in his career, Clough dropped deep and stroked the ball forward to Webb, who kept the momentum going by coaxing it out wide to the onrushing Carr. For once, Carr succeeded in not spooning the ball high over the goal but calmly passed the ball to Chapman who simply couldn't miss from six yards out. He didn't. Back at the City Ground, an extra tub of Brasso to clean another trophy was ordered. Forest would go on to claim the last Full Members' Cup in 1992 (by now the Zenith Data Systems Cup), beating Southampton 3-2 on a rain-sodden day in a predictably pulsating final. With English clubs (apart from Liverpool) allowed back into European competitions for the 1990/91 season, this sideshow of a competition's days were numbered.

The European ban denied this exciting Brian Clough team a few shots at Europe, including the UEFA Cup in 1988/89 for finishing third, again in 89/90 for another third-place finish and for lifting the League Cup and just for good measure, again in 90/91 for retaining the League Cup. Bitterly disappointing but lifting a trophy at Wembley helped to put a few smiles on a few faces.

Parker went on to see off the challenge of John Sheridan for his place after the club sold Webb, and he also partnered Roy Keane before leaving for Aston Villa in 1991 after scoring 17 goals in 103 appearances. A spell with Leicester City followed where he made the acquaintance of Neil Lennon who, since moving into management, employed Parker as a coach at Celtic and Bolton Wanderers.

He is fondly remembered at Forest though, none more so than by Brian Laws, with whom he remains close. 'I've been very lucky to play with some great players, but my closest friend was probably Garry Parker at Nottingham Forest,' Laws told Czech website Czech Forest. 'We came in at the same time and went through the processes that everyone else had to – in terms of waiting our turn to get into the first team. We played a lot of reserve team football prior to that and gelled together. Our friendship is still there now.

'We keep in touch regularly. He is probably one of my closest friends in football.'

In 2010, when working for Celtic, Parker suffered a mini-stroke while recuperating at home from a broken leg sustained while playing in a veterans' game.

Parker, then 44, told the *Daily Record*, 'I was in shock about the whole thing, especially the mini-stroke. I was back home having a kip and my wife Petra noticed one side of my face had dropped. She had seen the TV campaign and recognised the signs immediately. If she had not been so quick I could have died or been left disabled. She was great.

'But you have to put everything into perspective. I had treatment in the John Radcliffe Hospital, which is where they do post-mortems on the lads who have died in Afghanistan. I saw the bodies come in and you value even more what they are doing. I just have to get on with it. If I have to take tablets for the rest of my life so be it.'

Parker didn't quite get the recognition he deserved but he was perfect for this team: a nice young man who could play football extremely well. If Paul Gascoigne had received the appropriate punishment for stamping his studs into Parker's chest before scything down Gary Charles in the 1991 FA Cup Final, perhaps he would have an FA Cup winner's medal too. However, he will always be fondly remembered for this goal and that belter at Bristol, making a fundamental contribution to the history of Nottingham Forest.

'I've smashed it into the net. It sounds simple really!' Colin Barrett hammers the ball past Liverpool captain Emlyn Hughes (right) to score Nottingham Forest's second goal during their European Cup first round, first leg match at the City Ground on 13 September 1978. (Getty Images.)

'My life changed from the moment I got on the end of John Robertson's cross.' Trevor Francis dives forward to head the winning goal. (Getty Images)

'It was great – a fantastic feeling.' John Robertson shoots to secure a second consecutive European Cup as Ian Bowyer moves out of the path of the shot. (Getty Images)

'The best goal I ever scored in my career.' Steve Hodge dives to score Nottingham Forest's second goal during the UEFA Cup semi-final first leg against Anderlecht at the City Ground, 11 April 1984. (Getty Images)

Nigel Clough celebrates after scoring the third goal for Forest in a 3-0 victory against Tottenham Hotspur on 24 October 1987. This was one of 131 goals he scored for the club, making him the second highest scorer in the club's history. (Getty Images)

Nottingham Forest's Neil Webb celebrating after scoring his side's goal in the FA Cup semi-final at Old Trafford on 7 May 1990. (Getty Images)

Roy Keane exchanges words with Spurs' Justin Edinburgh during a heated confrontation during the 1991 FA Cup Final. (Getty Images)

Scot Gemmill shoots to score the first of his two goals in the Zenith Data Systems Cup Final at Wembley on 29 March 1992. (Getty Images)

Denis Irwin and Gary Pallister try in vain to prevent Stan Collymore from scoring during an FA Carling Premiership match at Old Trafford. Forest won the match 2-1. (Anton Want/Allsport)

Stuart Pearce celebrates after scoring his shoot-out penalty past Spain goalkeeper Andoni Zubizarreta during the 1996 European Championships quarter-final match victory against Spain at Wembley Stadium on 22 June 1996. (Getty Images)

Chris Bart-Williams in action during the FA Carling Premiership match against Blackburn Rovers played at Ewood Park on 8 May 1999. (Ross Kinnaird /Allsport)

Steve Chettle proudly captains his boyhood team in the Nationwide Division One match against Walsall at the City Ground. (Phil Cole/Allsport)

Nottingham born and bred, Wesley Morgan celebrates against Charlton Athletic at the City Ground on 6 January 2007. (Getty Images)

'His face was thunderous with joy.' Stuart Pearce celebrates his team's first goal during the Sky Bet Championship match between Derby County and Nottingham Forest at iPro Stadium on 17 January 2015. (Getty Images)

Dexter Blackstock in classic 'towering far-post header after a good old-fashioned bout of clambering and wrestling with an out-of-position full-back' pose battles with Patrick Bauer of Charlton Athletic during the Sky Bet Championship match between Nottingham Forest and Charlton Athletic at the City Ground on 18 August 2015. (Getty Images)

Chris Cohen celebrates after scoring to make it 2-0 during the crucial Sky Bet Championship match between Nottingham Forest and Ipswich Town at the City Ground on 7 May 2017.
(Getty Images)

Neil Webb vs
Luton Town (1989)

I F it wasn't for Neil Webb, Brian Clough's trophy collection might have been sparser than it eventually was. It if wasn't for Neil Webb, Sir Alex Ferguson may well be plain old Alex Ferguson, also known as that Scottish guy who couldn't quite cut it south of the border.

A full nine years had passed since Clough's mantelpiece groaned under the weight of a significant trophy, until Webb swept in a Tommy Gaynor pass to score a decisive goal in the 1989 League Cup Final. More trophies would follow thick and fast for Clough's second great Forest team that enjoyed more days at Wembley than a number 224 London bus.

It was Webb who picked out the gallivanting Lee Martin in the 1990 FA Cup Final, who promptly dispatched the ball past Nigel Martyn for Manchester United to claim their first silverware under Ferguson. The East Stand goalposts at Wembley brought the best from Webb and in doing so, provided his bosses with valuable trophies and medals.

Having etched his name into Reading's history books by becoming their youngest ever goalscorer aged 17 years and 31 days, Webb moved on to Portsmouth until his goalscoring exploits from midfield caught the attention of Nottingham Forest. Clough's trusted lieutenants, Alan Hill and Liam O'Kane, travelled up and down from Nottingham to the south coast on numerous scouting missions. As O'Kane recalled in Nottingham Forest periodical *Bandy and Shinty*, 'Portsmouth and back, every other week. And he was crap, every time.'

Clough wasn't dissuaded. Webb signed for Forest in 1985 and got down to doing what he did best for the best part of the next four years: weaving pretty triangles before scoring goals from midfield, his first being on his debut at Luton Town's Kenilworth Road on the opening day of the season in a 1-1 draw.

It was a significant summer for the club in terms of recruitment since alongside Webb, in walked Brian Rice from Hibernian and Stuart Pearce from Coventry City. Furthermore, Nigel Clough was about to start his first full season after making his debut in the previous one, just like Des Walker. The foundations were being laid for an exciting few years ahead.

Despite Webb notching on his debut, lessons had to be learned. He was working for Brian Clough and no matter how talented a player may be, there was a right way and a wrong way to play football in Clough's team. Everyone had to learn this. Some learned easily; others took more time.

Webb got the gist of Clough's requirements soon enough though. 'In his first full game with us Webb attempted some kind of fancy cross from the touchline and succeeded only in flipping the ball out of play,' Clough wrote in his autobiography. 'So I dragged him off, sending on a substitute instead. I told him that it was hard enough trying to play the ball normally without attempting to chip the bloody thing from that kind of position.'

The badgering and cajoling of Webb from his boss wasn't confined to just that one lesson either. Pearce recounts, 'He (Clough) switched his attention to Webby who was much more a couple of glasses of wine man that I ever was. Maybe because Neil had cost the most, Clough gave him no respite; he hammered him. He was on his case all the time as if he was trying to make or break him.'

If Clough did indeed hammer him, it was clearly because he liked what he saw and knew the boy could play. Moreover, he didn't break Webby, who just got on with spraying balls hither and thither, usually into the feet of the number nine who dropped deep, thus creating space for Webb to exploit.

His goalscoring record at Forest – just short of one every three games – remains deeply impressive. It's little wonder that he eventually won his boss over. When Steve Hodge returned to the club looking to win back his place in the middle of the park, he found that his old boss had a new teacher's pet. In his first game back at Norwich City, Clough told Hodge at half-time, 'Harry darling. When you get the ball, give it to Neil Webb. He's a good midfield player.'

With Webb pulling the strings, Forest made steady progress in the coming seasons with consecutive eighth-place finishes before then finishing third in successive years. It was in Webb's fourth season – 1988/89 – that the club had something tangible to show for their pretty passing patterns by claiming not only the Simod Cup but also one of Clough's favourites, the League Cup.

Thanks to one of Garry Parker's timely blockbusting shots in biblical rain at Ashton Gate, Forest found themselves in their first major final since the victorious European Cup of 1980. Just a few weeks previously, Everton had been disposed of at Wembley in a thrilling Simod Cup Final but in truth, this was the one that really mattered. At this time, Luton were no pushovers and had the League Cup under lock and key having defeated Arsenal in an epic final the previous year.

Clough's young charges were faltering in the first half in front of 76,310. They were a blossoming team and perhaps a little overwhelmed. Mick Harford nodded the Hatters into a lead and Forest made the long stroll to the Wembley dressing rooms a goal down. 'We were nervous in the first half but there was no ranting or raving at half-time,' Webb recalled in *Wembley Again!* 'The gaffer simply reminded us that we were better than that, and that we had to show it.'

Wise and simple words that the situation demanded – effective too. Webb and his young scamps set about playing football like they had done for the previous four seasons. Hodge burst into the penalty area after a defence-splitting pass from Webb but was felled by Les Sealey, and Clough stroked the penalty home.

The cork was off. The team breathed again. Forest were in the ascendency, yet they needed another goal to take the lead and break Luton's stranglehold on the trophy. The door was ajar; it just needed breaking down.

⚽ ⚽ ⚽

Clough has the scent of victory. He and strike partner Lee Chapman contrive to win the ball in their own half from a dawdling Luton midfielder. Clough wins the tackle, Chapman has the ball and he feeds it wide right to Tommy Gaynor, who motors upfield. The break is on.

Clough runs forward. Chapman does the same but Webb is the furthest forward. Gaynor spies him and sweeps a deliciously curving ball over the back-pedalling defence and into his path 12 yards from goal. With one touch of his left boot, he brings it under control.

With another touch of his right, the ball is beyond Sealey and Forest are well on their way to claiming their first major piece of silverware since the miracle years: the first for Clough without his mate Peter Taylor, the first for Clough senior with his lad in the team. From Clough winning the ball to Webb scoring, a mere 12 seconds elapse.

Life comes at you fast in a Wembley cup final.

⚽ ⚽ ⚽

'Tommy Gaynor made a great run and had a great first touch to put it in his path,' recalled Webb. 'As soon as he made that though I thought, "That's it, I'm going." I just ran. I didn't look to see if I was offside, I was just thinking if he puts the cross in I'm going to be on the end of it and he put a great cross in and I took it down. Les Sealey came out "flat" so when I touched it I just had to flick it over him and into the net.

'I never, ever got a feeling like that, and of course it was in front of the Forest fans at that end as well. When I put it in I just ran and jumped over some advertising boards as well and when I turned round you could just see it on my face, I couldn't believe I'd just scored in a major cup final at Wembley in front of my own fans.'

Young Clough would seal the win with a calm finish to give the score-line a lovely touch of gloss and claim the man of the match prize. Webb's display was heralded as one of many impressive performances during the season. Amid the euphoric scenes, Webb found the time to show just how much of a nice young Cloughean disciple he had become. Steve Sutton remembers, 'Neil ran half the length of the pitch to shake hands with me, which was nice.'

The vultures were circling. Such progress and success doesn't go unnoticed. A reliable goalscoring midfielder was and always will be on the shopping list of any club that has aspirations of winning titles. Manchester United were exactly that club and come the summer after the League Cup win, Webb was off to Old Trafford to follow in the footsteps of Ian Storey-Moore, Garry Birtles and Peter Davenport.

All went swimmingly at Old Trafford. Or at least it did to begin with. Just like he did on his Forest debut, Webb got his name on the scoresheet by slamming one in on the volley to secure a 3-1 opening day win against Arsenal.

Bad luck lurked around the corner though, and just a few months later, he snapped his Achilles tendon while playing for England against Sweden. This was a cruel twist of fate to deliver to a Forest player trying to make his name at Manchester United yet given Davenport's and Birtles's experiences, this dose of unlucky potion number 13 was probably to be expected. This put a dent not only in his progress at Old Trafford but also his England career and his hopes of adding to his 27 caps and four goals.

His debut for England as a 64th-minute substitute for Glenn Hoddle in a friendly against West Germany in Düsseldorf in 1987 was a significant moment, since it meant he was the 1,000th player in history to be capped for England. It was while plying his trade at Forest that international recognition came his way, and naturally his boss had something to say about Webb's progress.

Clough said, 'We taught Webb his game. We taught him how to become a midfield player because, at first, he didn't tackle enough. When I asked him his first job in midfield he spluttered and looked confused, so I told him, "Your first job is to get the ball, because we can't play without it." Eventually we got him into the England side – as we did with so many others.'

Webb's return to the City Ground with his new friends didn't come until the end of the season – Forest's final home game to be specific. Webb had missed United's crucial third round FA Cup tie there earlier in the season owing to that injury sustained on international duty. This is the game surrounded in myth that apparently, were Mark Robins not to have nodded United's only goal, Alex Ferguson would have been out on his ear.

Webb's return to Trentside could not be put off though and on a blazing hot day in May, Webb and his team were humiliated 4-0 and despite lifting the FA Cup, ended up a deeply underwhelming 13th in the league. Just four days earlier, Forest had successfully retained the League Cup by seeing off a stubborn Oldham Athletic thanks to a goal from Nigel Jemson.

Among Forest fans, the consensus was that Webb had left the club purely for financial gain. After all, the team Webb left had just lifted the League Cup and finished third in the league while Manchester United trailed in 11th place. Various Forest fanzines, most prominently *Brian* and *The Tricky Tree* dubbed Webb 'Fat Wallet'.

'Stuart Pearce used to get one of the fanzines, *The Tricky Tree*, and they were bloody terrible to me,' recounted Webb in Daniel Taylor's *Deep Into The Forest*. 'I got absolutely hammered. It was understandable, I suppose, because the fans felt I had let them down but I still wasn't quite prepared for how bad it actually was. Sometimes you can blank out the supporters but not when it's constant abuse from the first whistle to the last.'

Anyone who thinks that footballers are robots and should simply get on with what they are paid handsomely to do perhaps needs to recalibrate their thinking. Webb said, 'I didn't think it would affect me. But it did. Every time I got the ball I was nervous because I felt I had to do something good and because of that I ended up giving it away more often than not. It was one of my worst games for Man U and we lost 4-0.'

Webb wasn't utterly broken though and a month later, he delivered the assist for Lee Martin's epoch-creating goal at Wembley. Yet with Paul Ince, Bryan Robson and Lee Sharpe vying for places in the middle of the park and Paul Scholes, David Beckham and Nicky Butt waiting in the wings, starting places in the United midfield were at a premium.

Webb returned to the City Ground in 1992 but despite starring in a 4-1 win at Elland Road in December he could do nothing to prevent Forest finishing bottom of the pile.

He made nine appearances in the relegation season and many forget that he played 21 games in the subsequent promotion season under Frank Clark and weighed in with three goals. Once promoted though, he fell from favour and although he never played again for the club, he remained contracted for another two years.

There is little doubt that Webb found retirement from the game difficult yet for many Forest fans, he is forever strolling around the midfield in his second generation Airstrike Nike boots with the distinctive yellow lettering around the heel and the prominent swoosh with either Home Ales or Shipstones on his chest playing neat triangles with Pearce before laying the ball into Clough's feet and bombing forward for a return, which he nonchalantly dispatches goalbound – sometimes in a major cup final too.

His eye for a goal or a sweeping pass kick-started a trophy glut for both Alex Ferguson and Brian Clough. It is for precisely this that Neil Webb deserves to be remembered.

Gary Crosby vs
Manchester City (1990)

GEORGE Best did it. Robin van Persie did it. Thierry Henry did it. Ronaldinho did it. Gary Crosby did it. Arguably, Crosby did it better than all the rest too since what separates him from those above is that his effort counted.

Affectionately known as 'Meatfly', owing to his slight frame, or perhaps less original but more memorably, 'Bing', Crosby seemed to pop up at the right time when Forest were pounding a well-beaten path to Wembley in the late 1980s. Signed from Grantham Town in 1987 having made only 12 appearances while plying his trade under Martin O'Neill, Crosby went on to make 152 appearances for Forest, scoring 12 goals in the process.

Quiff quivering in the wind like an English Pat Nevin, Crosby frequently made right-backs look like they were re-enacting a Chubby Checker song as he darted this way then that before invariably side-footing a ball into the penalty area for his mate, Nigel Clough, to stroke into the net.

He could finish too. On a bittersweet day at Birmingham City in the 1988 FA Cup fifth round tie on which violence outside the ground is the abiding memory for most Forest fans, it was Crosby who drove his shot beyond Blues keeper Roger Hansbury after a through ball from Clough to earn the Reds a quarter-final date against Arsenal at Highbury.

It was Crosby too who bagged the opening goal a year later, again, in the FA Cup semi-final against West Ham United at Villa Park. Again, it is perhaps a game overshadowed by other events, this time Keith Hackett's decision to send off Irons defender Tony Gale for what he deemed to be a professional foul on, of course, Crosby. New rules came into force a few days before this game and since, at least in Hackett's eyes, Gale denied Crosby a clear scoring opportunity when he tugged his shoulder back as the winger wriggled free of him, he saw red.

Since football is football, it was Crosby who poked in the opening goal in a 4-0 win after delightful approach play. Ian Woan picked out Clough in the middle of the park who then dinked the ball past Martin Allen in a move so beautiful that Allen simply gave up playing football there and then. Clough lay the ball to his right since when Roy Keane has made a run to get up there, you tended to pass the ball to him. Keane was challenged so squared the ball even further to the right for the onrushing Crosby, who took a touch and stroked the ball beyond Luděk Mikloško. Forest were on their way to a first FA Cup final since 1959.

And yet, despite the significance of these two goals, it is the one he scored in an otherwise forgettable league game against Manchester City that would be the one for which he is remembered – an ultimately mid-table humdrum encounter in a season in which Forest would finish ninth and their opponents 14th.

⚙ ⚙ ⚙

Like most good things, it starts with Garry Parker who, having been fed by first Terry Wilson then Nigel Jemson, swings a ball in from the right. With only perhaps the league's smallest players in Steve Hodge and Crosby anywhere near the penalty area, it is, in retrospect, difficult to see what Parker was trying to achieve.

Any goalkeeper worth their salt – and Andy Dibble is indeed one of those – would pluck it out of the air and do that fall to the floor thing that goalkeepers do when they want to bring the ball fully under their control. This Dibble does.

Steve Hodge goes in for a nibble but quickly retreats when he sees the ball is firmly in Dibble's grasp. Dibble gets to his feet, goes to throw a short one to his right-back but thinks better of it and holds the ball in his right hand, chewing nonchalantly. His right-back Alan Harper darts past him – Dibble gives him a quick glance but thinks nothing of it. He holds the ball in his right hand – palm facing towards the sky. The ball rests on it, as beautiful and tempting as the Fertility Idol that Indiana Jones steals and replaces with a bag of sand in *Raiders of the Lost Ark*.

Crosby can't help himself. He has no bag of sand but he's not concerned with replacing the ball, just stealing it. So he does exactly that – he nods the ball from Dibble's upturned palm and taps it into the Bridgford End goal.

While Crosby scampers back to the safety of his team-mates with the expression of one who's just placed a whoopee cushion on the supply teacher's chair – outwardly serious but inside, giddy with joy which will be released only when he is certain he has got away with it, Dibble is busy absolutely losing it in the manner of someone who's just been passed on to a third anonymous voice at a call centre having been told that 'it's out of their hands'.

He runs out of his area, pursuing referee Rodger Gifford as if he's about to chop him up into small pieces with a plastic spork. Yet he suddenly stops. He knows that not just Gifford but the game of football and indeed, the universe has conspired against him and there is nothing he can do about it.

He mumbles 'fuck' to no one in particular. He prowls while Gary Megson, Peter Reid and City manager Howard Kendall argue the case, still intent on committing all manner of bad things on Crosby. Yet when he sees Gifford run to the centre of the pitch in that way referees do when they have made their mind up and just want everyone to get on with the game, he knows it's happened. It is already history. It can't unhappen.

He slams the floor in disgust with the world for allowing this to happen. He is one step away from full-on, unadulterated toddler writhing around in aisle three of the supermarket screaming, 'It's not fair.'

On commentary duty, a pre-Sky Martin Tyler seems to struggle to see what Dibble's beef is, 'well the ball was only resting on one hand. Was it in his grasp? The referee said "no". Dibble had the ball resting on the palm of his right hand but that, Gary Crosby realised, wasn't in full control of the ball.'

❂ ❂ ❂

An otherwise unremarkable game had just got remarkable. For his post-match interview, Tyler dragged Kendall on to a freezing cold City Ground pitch to vent his spleen. 'I mean I can't believe it. Was it George Best that knocked the ball out of Gordon Banks's hands about 25 years ago? And that was disallowed. Have we not improved since then?' said Kendall.

Tyler reiterated the point he made in commentary that perhaps Dibble wasn't in full control of the ball. Kendall stared into the distance. He paused, 'What...with the ball in his hand?'

Tyler would not let it go. 'In ONE hand.'

Kendall again stared away into the void, looking for all the world as if he could actually weep real tears live on television. He couldn't believe this cruel, harsh and unforgiving world had denied his team a point and moreover this cruel, harsh and unforgiving world was now seemingly ganging up and pointing fingers at him, constantly reminding him that his goalkeeper only had the ball in 'one hand'.

In a changing room close by, a goalkeeper was either sat staring at this upturned palm or systematically smashing every piece of furniture in the room. Maybe both.

Kendall went into full-on 'present a spurious argument that makes little sense then and even less sense 30 years later' mode, 'Oh dearie me. Is a handball with one hand or is it with two hands? If you're stopping play for a handball, you don't use two hands do you? You use one hand. The ball is in the keeper's hands. There's no way that that is a goal.'

In a foreshadow of his future opinion-offering self, Gary Lineker gave his verdict, 'I've seen it a few times and I still can't

123

really make my mind up. Errrm...you've got to give full credit to Gary Crosby though – he just heads it out of his hand and knocks it in. Some refs, I think most refs would probably have disallowed it. I don't think there's an actual rule.'

Lineker would spend the next 30 years working on offering more erudite, coherent and left-leaning opinions.

It was all kicking off in the ITV studio as they prepared to cover another live game elsewhere. World Cup referee George Courtney was seemingly doorstepped and asked, 'Would you have given that goal?'

'No.' His reply was as gruff and firm as a slab of northern rock.

Reluctantly, he elucidated, 'In the spirit of the game, I wouldn't have allowed it. It's the first time I've seen that in nearly 30 years of refereeing – I've never come across it. The law, or the letter of the law, doesn't accommodate for a goal in that way but in the spirit of the laws, I wouldn't have allowed it.'

So wait. Hang on. There is nothing in the laws to rule against the goal? Is that what you're saying? That according to the laws, as they stand, the goal stands?

That seemed to be the case. Danny Baker interpreted the situation similarly and with glee and confidence declared, 'It's a perfectly good goal.'

Next up was Jimmy Greaves, perched in some gantry high up in a stand feeling cheerful since Crosby's goal had momentarily diverted his mind away from the Siberian wind that was clearly causing him some discomfort. Greaves comes at the issue from an entirely logical perspective – the ex-striker's. 'Against the spirit of the game? I can't see it personally.'

No time for any dressed-up flowery prose or chicanery such as 'spirit of the game' nonsense. He debunked that myth straightaway and then warmed to his theme.

Greaves continued, 'Keepers are an overprotected species as you know. The ball comes in and as far as I'm concerned, it's a wonderful piece of ingenuity by the player who makes no contact with the goalkeeper whatsoever. He sees the keeper with the ball held out. He heads it out of his hands. It's no more than taking the ball off a full-back's foot and putting it in the back of the net and that's what Crosby did. I think that the referee did the right thing – it was a very bold decision but what a great goal for all goalscorers! Lovely!'

And he was right wasn't he? Perhaps not in drawing an analogy with nicking the ball from a full-back – that part doesn't quite work. But right there – in that final word. 'Lovely.' That is precisely where Greaves got right to the heart of the matter.

Football is about moments. Moments that stay with those who saw them for the rest of their lives. In most cases, such moments are goals. Simply put, football is goals and it is lovely so see them, regardless of how they are scored. In fact, the more unusual, the better.

Once in a while, a player will find a new way to score a goal and as long as it is within the rules of the game, it's legal, well that's just lovely.

Dibble put on a brave face moving on. 'The worst thing is that I've got a sponsored car as well and that makes it hard. I get people driving past me and giving it one of them [mimics Crosby's head movement] but to me it's gone now, it's history and it's out of my life,' he said.

In the subsequent Forest matchday programme, Crosby admitted, 'In hindsight it was controversial, but it was just one of those things that football throws up every so often. It wasn't a premeditated thing. It was a total split second, spur of the moment incident and I hope no one connected with Manchester City still harbours any bad feelings about it.'

If it's any consolation to City fans – which it isn't – Forest would not taste victory for another eight games yet they would lift the League Cup for the second successive year against Oldham Athletic.

The spoilsports at the FA ensured this sort of thing would never happen again and denied us van Persie, Henry and Ronaldinho's similar Crosby-esque efforts counting for anything.

Gary Crosby – the imp that got away with something Best, van Persie, Henry and Ronaldinho couldn't.

Scot Gemmill vs Arsenal (1991)

COMMON consensus states that once Stan Collymore walked through the door in 1993 after Forest had tumbled rather unceremoniously out of the inaugural Premier League, he single-handedly sharp-shot them back to the top tier.

Sure, Stuart Pearce weighed in with some vital goals – most famously one at Peterborough United's London Road – and obviously Frank Clark did well too in keeping his nerve and steadying the ship after a less than convincing start of just two wins from the opening ten games. But it was Stan who did it, wasn't it?

Like many things, though, it's not as simple as that and besides, simply swallowing 'common consensus' has on occasions got society into pickles bigger than a Branston factory.

Returning to the Premier League at the first time of asking was and remains a very big deal. Were this not to have been achieved, kiss goodbye to that subsequent record-breaking third-place finish the following season. Collymore's goal at Old Trafford evaporates into a puff of smoke. Another crack at Europe in the UEFA Cup remains more elusive than a wasted ball from Xavi.

So while returning at the fist time of asking was perhaps an even bigger achievement than understood at the time, it wasn't all about Collymore. Although he did indeed top-score that season with 24 goals – 19 in the league – and did indeed, on occasions, seem to go out and win games single-handedly

(West Bromwich Albion and Sunderland away spring readily to mind), it was a 46-game season and there was a very talented supporting cast.

Besides, Scot Gemmill was just behind Collymore in the leading scorer stakes that season: one more than Colin Cooper, two more than Pearce and three more than Lee Glover, Steve Stone and Ian Woan. Gemmill made 30 appearances that season and scored a goal almost every third game he played.

Yet for all of this, Gemmill was and remains somewhat under-appreciated. Maybe it's because he didn't run very fast. Maybe it's because he had floppy hair and one particular curly lock frequently got in his eyes. Maybe it's because his dad drove his pregnant wife, Betty, north of the border for Scot's birth so that he would be eligible to represent the country for which Archie scored that barely plausible goal against Holland. Maybe it's because his name is spelled with just the one 't' since it's short for Scotland. Maybe it's because he is ever so slightly different from your average top-flight footballer.

Not every dressing room is packed with footballers who have an appreciation of the Brooklyn-based Jose Parla, specialist in exploring the boundary between abstraction and calligraphy. He told *Herald Scotland*, 'When I stopped playing my wife, Ruth, and I decided to stay in New York for six months. I am a big fan of Parla and we visited his studio. One night we were walking back to our apartment and there was this surreal moment. There was a painting lying against the wall of a building. It was just discarded, lying there. But it was not there by accident.'

So what does Gemmill do after spying such a piece produced by an acclaimed artist? He picks it up and takes it home. Obviously.

'I am certain it is a Parla. It is hanging in our house now,' he said.

Of course, he does. That's precisely the kind of thing Gemmill does. Just like he played football, he saw something no one else did, took a risky yet brave option and produced a special moment.

Sure, he had a famous dad but he wasn't the only player in the dressing room in that situation – some lad called Nigel had a father who was also a pretty big deal at Forest. Yet Gemmill was always sanguine about that. 'My father was so successful that I judge myself against him but I was never the star player, never the fans' favourite.

'I lived a completely normal life even though I was a Premiership footballer. I could walk down the street completely unrecognised,' he said.

'People ask me what's it's like to have a famous father? I don't know what it's like not to have a famous father. It's completely normal to me to have a famous father. But I know it's affected me. It's influenced the way I behave as a coach and how I am as a person. It's all connected to him.'

Forest was a family club and his future boss had known young Gemmill since, well, before he was even knee-high to a grasshopper. Before he was even born as it happens. 'Gemmill's lovely wife, Betty, was heavily pregnant at the time, carrying Scot,' recalled Brian Clough in his autobiography. 'Little did I know then that the unborn bairn would actually be playing for me at Nottingham Forest by the time I closed the Clough managerial chapter.'

As the 1990s found their groove, Gemmill was handed his debut in March 1991 against Wimbledon at Plough Lane. The thought of young Scot going toe to toe with Keith Curle, Lawrie Sanchez, Carlton Fairweather and John Fashanu is enough to make you curl up in a brace position in fear for the lad. Such a debut reeks of Brian Clough – renowned for chucking young lads in at the deep end. He was rarely wrong though and as usual, Clough knew when a young player was ready.

The following season, Gemmill got down to the business of establishing himself in Clough's team, plundering 12 goals and helping Forest to eighth position in the table and a League Cup Final appearance against Manchester United. While Teddy Sheringham was the top scorer, Gemmill ended up joint second, level with Roy Keane.

The defeat to United at Wembley was a disappointing affair yet prior to that, a rain-soaked afternoon at the national stadium was enjoyed by Forest as they lifted the Full Members' Cup (Zenith Data System Cup) after a 3-2 victory against Southampton.

Gemmill opened the scoring with a thunderous volley from the edge of the area that found the top corner and had Tim Flowers beaten all ends, sides and bottoms up. Kingsley Black doubled the lead before the Saints finally popped the clutch, found a gear and drew level with goals from Matthew Le Tissier and Kevin Moore.

The game moved into extra time and Gemmill popped up at the far post to volley in a cross from Gary Charles. His star was on the rise.

Two weeks later, Forest were back at Wembley to contest the wretched League Cup Final against United and the following season would be Clough's final one.

Young Scot stuck around and if Collymore led from the front, Gemmill was one of those with a very steady foot holding the ladder. Memorably, Forest carved to pieces a very decent Leicester City side that would claim fourth place in the league on the way to promotion. Even without Collymore, Forest roared to a 4-0 win with young Scot bagging two goals – one of them designed to make opposition custodian Kevin Poole look a right old plonker as he returned his wayward clearance with interest from 40 yards.

Yet Gemmill's goal in a 3-2 victory against Arsenal in a league game at the City Ground in 1991/92 illustrates perfectly his deftness of touch.

Ian Woan fired the home team ahead with a typically Woan-like rising, rasping drive from an angle. As the second half played out, a creeping frost edged its way across the pitch as December kicked in. Sheringham doubled the lead. But Clough's young team wasn't done yet. Gemmill was about to take the stage.

⚽ ⚽ ⚽

Gary Crosby gallops forwards and lays the ball out to Gary Charles, who has burst forward from right-back and is ahead of his winger. This is classic Clough full-back play well before Cafu, Dani Alves and Pep Guardiola styled converted full-backs into midfielders. Charles nudges it towards Sheringham who is lurking just inside the penalty area with deadly intent. The shot's not on though, so he coaxes the ball ever so gently into the box for the onrushing Gemmill.

David Seaman senses danger and is out quick, bearing down on Gemmill like a big cuddly bear about to envelop a honey pot. Young Scot faces a decision: blast it and hope for the best? Yes. Go with that.

He shapes to blast it but then dinks it over Seaman, avoiding the big bear clinch that otherwise awaits him. The ball loops over the bear and bounces apologetically before it even reaches the line. It's that delicate. He kisses both hands and stretches them out in front of the old Trent End. Can he do it on a frozen pitch in December against Steve Bould and David Seaman? Sure. No worries. Of course he can. You don't get to play in Brian Clough's first team if you can't.

⚽ ⚽ ⚽

Paul Merson and then Alan Smith made Forest sweat but Gemmill's goal deserved to win the game, and was arguably one of the best of the whole season.

When you have bravery and a gossamer-light touch, pace and brawn is superfluous. Clough loved players like this and saw past their limitations in order to focus on what they *could* do. Team-mate and fellow Verve and Richard Ashcroft obsessive Paul McGregor valued this bravery, 'I love a natural player – ballers' ballers. Scot Gemmill was incredible with the ball – he just never gave it away. He was brave in different ways: you look at someone like Stuart Pearce who was brave going into the challenge but it's a lot braver to want the ball under pressure constantly.'

As you might expect from someone raised by Archie Gemmill and managed by Clough, young Scot carries such footballing values into his coaching career. He said, 'At Forest, there was no real coaching but the message was clear in regards of keeping the ball. Most of Clough's team-talks involved a towel in the middle of the dressing-room floor with the ball on it, the referee banging on the door, demanding the teams go into the tunnel but nobody was allowed to move or speak until Clough said, "Get the ball and when we get it, we keep it and pass it to our Nige."'

Yet it goes beyond the football pitch. Football is a game yet life is continuous. The values that Brian and Archie instilled in him remain, 'I would go further than that and say he [Clough] influenced me as a person. I grew up in his company and he did not let you get away with anything. You were not allowed to act inappropriately and that included the most simple things of saying please or thank you.'

Given young Scot's coaching of the Scotland under-17 and under-21 teams, expect some very pleasant and well-schooled young men instilled with footballing bravery to be flooding out from north of the border in the future.

Roy Keane vs Tottenham Hotspur (1992)

B EFORE the death stare directed towards a fellow pundit...
Before the gloriously ungovernable Brian Blessedesque
beard...

Before that memorable performance in the Champions
League semi-final in Turin in 1999...

Before Saipan...

Before all of this, Roy Keane was a rather magnificent
footballer for Nottingham Forest.

Roy Keane (his satisfyingly onomatopoeic name sounds like
a sharp double whammy to the chin) didn't so much play football
but prowled with purpose – a snarling ball of indignation
with tapering elbows and glowing red eyes like General Zod
protruding from (at least in his early days) a somewhat wiry
frame of sinew and muscle composed of little more than pints,
kebabs and passion pure as the driven snow.

Picture him now: he's in the grill of a referee with what seems
to be a varicose vein protruding from his temples.

Or he's standing over a prone Alf-Inge Håland in the style
of Samuel L. Jackson's Jules over Frank Whaley's Brett in *Pulp
Fiction* – incapacitated by fear; daring him – nay, double daring
him – to come within even a small European country's area
surface of him ever again.

Or he's absolutely committed to maintaining a never-ending
feud in the 1991 FA Cup Final with what looks like the kid who
dines out on being the stand-in for when one of the members
of fifth-rate 90s boy band 911 can't make it for the *Going Live!*

phone-in appearance – or who may well be Justin fucking Edinburgh.

Or he's telling Mick McCarthy to stick it up his bollocks on a pot-holed pitch in Japan and walking away from a World Cup he has yearned for because the preparation is crap and nobody appears to be thinking about how best to actually win some football matches.

He wasn't a balletic mover. He didn't glide like Cruyff or sexy-hip-swivel like Maradona. He clunked like the Tin Man, in need of regular squirts of oil from Dorothy's can.

Yet none of this really matters. Your reputation, how you look, how many Instagram hits you have, the colour of your boots, the ship you sailed in on – Keane couldn't give less of a fuck because he is all out of fucks to give.

All Keane cares about – all he ever cared about – was winning. This was apparent from the moment he was asked by his gaffer to try on a Forest shirt in the away dressing room at Anfield in August 1990. Despite Forest being a hefty sized pebble in Liverpool's shoe around the late 70s and early 80s, the club's record on Merseyside was and remains pretty woeful.

Keane was probably unaware of this and even if he did know, chances are he didn't give a fuck. This 19-year-old went out and started dishing out advice to his minder at right-back that evening – a seasoned professional, Brian Laws.

Who would give a debut to such a young man at such an age and in such circumstances? Only one man would.

Brian Clough's assistant, Liam O'Kane, told *Bandy and Shinty* how much Clough, '*loved* Keaney. Loved him. We were playing Arnold Town mid-week. Brian, again, "Is Keaney not playing?" I said no, he's on the bench. "Well tell Archie to put him on." I went back to Archie and said, "The gaffer wants Keaney on." Archie says "all right", but Archie's a funny little fucker. Stubborn, and he won't do it.

'"Come on, Arch," I said, "get him on. Our lives aren't gonna be worth living otherwise." I can see Cloughie staring daggers at us, with his arms folded. So Keaney comes on, and scores two – a couple of headers – and then a few weeks later he's starting at Anfield. No one had heard of him. But Brian knew he was ready.'

Of course he was ready. Keane had been ready for top-flight football for a long time. Besides, this Clough fella had already made a deep and long-lasting impression on the boy from Cork. In his autobiography, Keane recollects meeting the man whom he would later rate as the best manager he played for:

"Is he any good?" Clough asked [Ronnie] Fenton, pointing at me.

"He can play a bit, boss," Fenton replied.

"Okay, Ronnie, give 'em the money." Turning to our delegation, he added, "You can call me Brian. Now let's have a drink." Turning to me – and the dog – he snapped, "Except you, you call me Mr Clough." They broke the mould when they created this guy, I thought to myself.'

Scot Gemmill too testifies to the seemingly unlikely Brian and Roy love-in, 'At the end of the game, Clough would normally be on his knees, offering to untie Keane's boots for him, because he idolised Keane.' Same goes for Steve Hodge, 'One day, Cloughie came in and he was in a bad mood. He sat us down and one by one went down the line and gave us all abuse. Then he got to Keane at the end and he went, "Keaney, I love you, Irishman."'

That's not to say there weren't hiccups along the way in those developmental years. An errant back-pass, which cost Forest an FA Cup tie victory against Crystal Palace, led to a defining moment between the two uncompromising men. Team-mate Phil Starbuck saw that night how much it hurt Keane to have let his gaffer down, 'Back in the dressing room, there's no Roy and there's no Mister Clough.

'The next thing we know, Roy came into the dressing room and he's got tears in his eyes. It really hurt Roy – he was very dejected, head down, gutted.'

Clough had given Keane a whack in the stomach – a very tangible reminder that when you play for his football club, you play the right way and avoid doing 'owt daft. Maybe it didn't stop

Keane doing daft things off the football pitch but it certainly made him think twice about doing daft things on it.

By this stage, Clough had instilled into Keane a deep sense of loyalty. Keane was regularly given permission to fly home to Ireland after Saturday's game and not worry about showing his face until Monday morning and if he was a bit late back, it was no big deal. Had Clough gone soft as he entered the final phase of his magisterial management career?

Far from it. He was simply implementing the strategy that had served him well all his life – work out what the players need or don't need and let them get on with it. His faith in 'The Irishman' to do his job on the pitch was already unswerving.

The tears Keane cried that evening weren't tears of physical hurt but tears of disappointment in letting his gaffer down. He said, 'I've never forgotten what he did for me – and how he did it. He was his own man, prepared to be daring, at odds with the conventional wisdom of any given day. On the day of the Southampton game [Keane's home debut], Clough was particularly courteous to my family. For all his success Clough could be touchingly human, which is not too frequently the case with living legends.'

Even at this embryonic stage of his career, Keane had the habit of scoring big goals – goals that counted double; goals that really mattered, goals that were thinly coded messages for his will to win. FA Cup quarter-final? Goal away at Norwich. FA Cup semi-final? Goal against West Ham United. Yet perhaps his most glorious moment in Garibaldi red – the absolute embodiment of a 'fuck you and all of your poxy mates' goal – is his moment at a rain-sodden White Hart Lane on a memorable day in the capital.

Forest faced Spurs in the League Cup semi-final. With the first leg at the City Ground producing a 1-1 draw, Gary Lineker and his mob fancied their chances of inflicting only a barely believable second League Cup tie defeat in four years on Clough's young charges. Winners in 1989 and again in 1990, Coventry City eventually prised Forest's hypnotic grip on the trophy away later that year but not without the granddaddy of all fightbacks.

Four goals down, Forest replied with four of their own before succumbing to a disappointingly underwhelming winner from Cyrille Regis after some penalty area ping-pong.

A year down the line, Forest had the taste for more League Cup glory. Yet it wasn't just Tottenham Hotspur that stood in the way, the IRA too were an obstacle which Keane and his mates were required to overcome. On the day of the game a small device was discovered at White Hart Lane railway station. The expectant crowd sought shelter from the torrential rain in cafes, pubs and bus shelters. Eventually, the device was defused safely. Game on.

Lee Glover dug the ball out of a rain-sodden trench of mud in the Spurs penalty area to fire the Reds ahead but Gordon Durie curled over a bauble of a cross for Lineker to nod beyond Mark Crossley, who was perhaps preoccupied by the unfortunate combination of his yellow goalkeeper shirt and red shorts.

No. Not Tottenham. Not after the previous year's FA Cup Final. Not this way. Not after going ahead away from home. Not after standing outside in the cold, hard, unrelenting rain. Not now. Not again, but Forest stayed strong and made it to extra time.

❂ ❂ ❂

Gary Crosby hammers in a corner from the right. A gaggle of bodies is drawn towards the flight of the ball like iron filings to a magnet. One man stands apart from the rest and times his run with clockwork precision. He barely rises – he doesn't need to, owing to the force of the delivery and his own textbook body position upon meeting the ball.

The satisfying *thunk* of wet leather on a rock hard surface reverberates around the ground. A split second later, Erik Thorstvedt is sat in a puddle of mud while Keane is scaring the living shit out of the ecstatic Forest fans in celebration.

❂ ❂ ❂

Keane loved a goal celebration in these formative years. His was a kind of inverse Munchean scream — all wide-mouthed shouting in defiance of the universe to deny him victory. There was that one time at Norwich when he blotted his copybook and performed a little forward roll after scoring the winner in an FA Cup quarter-final. Yet even his most basic of dainty gymnastic moves was hard as nails. Besides, Clough called him out on it and he never did such a thing again.

That moment at White Hart Lane was a foreshadow of Turin where he dragged his Manchester United team back from the brink and a two-goal deficit to the European Cup Final while knowing he wouldn't participate in it owing to a second yellow card. Hard. As. Nails.

That's for the FA Cup Final. *That's* for Des Walker. *That's* for denying my gaffer the only major trophy he didn't get to stick on his mantelpiece. *That's* for Brian. Have it and keep it. Stick it up your bollocks.

It couldn't last. Manchester United were on the rise and defeated Forest in a bad-tempered and turgid final. A year later, Forest and Clough were on the ropes and out of the Premier League at precisely the wrong time. Sir Alex Ferguson knew Keane was the man to lead his fledglings and swooped. Keane was gone. Clough was gone. Turn your back for a moment and football kicks you in the nutsack.

This wasn't a case of Keane leaving his club in the lurch though. Despite knowing that he would leave for bigger and better things, Keane kept fighting (in the right way) throughout the relegation season. In his autobiography, Clough noted, 'The confidence of the young players dipped. Scot Gemmill's goals dried up. My son Nigel had a thin time too. Only Roy Keane was doing his stuff regularly.'

And that's precisely what he did for the rest of his career right in the very thick of the hurly-burly of the Premier League and the European Cup.

Keane was forged in Nottingham alongside Pearce and Clough. 'There are people who call themselves professionals, but in Stuart Pearce we had a player who really gave meaning to the word,' he eulogises. 'Pearce was a leader, a real pro.'

He loved Forest too. Still does as a matter of fact, 'The City Ground and Forest fans will always have a special place in my heart.'

Stuart Pearce vs
Manchester City (1992)

T O the wider footballing community, Stuart Pearce will perhaps be defined by one moment – one that occurred in that heady, giddy and fizzing summer of 1996 on 22 June. After a grinding and goalless battle with Spain to decide who would contest the Euro 96 semi-final, Pearce purposefully makes his way to the penalty area to take England's third penalty. He is calm. He is focused. He is not going to be rushed. He takes the time to clear the penalty spot of debris. He starts his run-up and...you know what happened next.

Andoni Zubizarreta never really stood a chance.

A nation breathed again. Everyone wanted him to score after...again, you know what.

The England-supporting public expressed their joy and relief. The Nottingham Forest-supporting brethren wept tears of pride.

He was more than a thundering, thunderbolting, swash-buckling, thunderbastard blasting, steel-thighed left-back. Those who had watched him since his debut in 1985 – all tight shorts and streaked blonde hair in a style somewhere between Euromullet and bowl on the head so mum can make a neat fringe and sides – had seen this type of thing before.

Sure, he could spank a ball with more force than a scorned housewife of the 1950s beating a rug. Clearly, he could hoist an unassuming right-winger into the laps of spectators in row K with a shoulder-barge or sliding tackle – just ask poor old Paul Reid of Leicester City who clearly must have done something unspeakably heinous to Pearce to deserve the unadulterated barbarous punishment meted out to him in a League Cup tie in 1988. Maybe he stole a chip from his plate while uttering, 'Just checking they're ok for you.' Frankly, if he did this, he was fair game.

But there was something else that Pearce could do exceptionally well – he could play football. You didn't get to be a mainstay in a Brian Clough side for eight years or so without being able to control and pass a ball; Gary Megson and John Sheridan could attest to this. In Clough's mid-to-late-80s side comprising of straight-backed young men with neat hair and lovely smiles, Pearce's appearance did jar a little – a bit like Craig Logan in Bros. Yet in terms of footballing aesthetic, he epitomised everything that Clough wanted in a footballer: brave on the ball, leadership and the ability to pass the ball forward accurately.

Nottingham Forest's relegation from the newly inaugurated Premier League in 1992/93 started about as well as it possibly could when Teddy Sheringham smashed in to the top corner to seal a 1-0 win against Liverpool. Everything was going to be glorious: the development of the Bridgford End would be completed soon, the Full Members' Cup was safely tucked away in the old cabinet, the club was looking forward to building on both an eighth-place finish and a League Cup Final appearance and what's more, they sported a quite lovely new pinstripe shirt.

Few could foresee the club going a painful ten games without a win on that perfect sunny August day, a run including six straight defeats to follow Sheringham's winner.

Come early October, Pearce and his team dragged their battered morale up to Maine Road. Things had picked up slightly with two draws to follow the six defeats and City themselves weren't pulling up any trees at this stage, even though they no doubt fancied doing exactly that against a struggling Forest team featuring no less than Carl Tiler, Ray McKinnon and Thorvaldur Örlygsson.

After 83 minutes, City were 2-1 ahead owing to goals from definitive 90s footballers Rick Holden and Fitzroy Simpson. McKinnon had bagged an equaliser in between and for his efforts, he received a bizarre celebratory right-hook-cum-fist-pump from Roy Keane, which came within a whisker of connecting.

By this stage, Pearce and his defence had conceded so many goals (21 in nine games) that defeat looked inevitable. Indeed, they had shipped five in one game against Oldham Athletic (who would only survive on goal difference come the final shakedown). In addition, the official striding around in the middle of the park just happened to be one Roger Milford. Talk about the odds being stacked against you.

So, when your goalkeeper rolls the ball out to you in the left-back position with only seven minutes remaining in which to salvage something from the game in the midst of a miserable run, the logical thing to do would be to use your Thor's hammer of a left foot and whack the ball upfield for a knock-down, a scrap, a hope in hell's chance of something – anything – happening. Anything.

No…not Pearce. *Keep it on the deck in my team, young man.*

⚽⚽⚽

So he does. Initially, he thinks about knocking it down the line but nothing's on. What to do? He turns back inside and lays it off to Scot Gemmill. Most left-backs in the early 90s would feel that at this stage, their job was complete.

Stand back and wait for a stray attacker to wander behind you and then raise your hand to the sky to appeal for offside. Not Pearce. He runs.

No. Actually, he doesn't run. He powers forward like a John Deere 4WD/Track Tractor and while young Gemmill has beautifully pirouetted around, he's well into the centre circle and Keith Curle is already wishing he had tracked Gary Bannister rather than face this behemoth bearing down on him.

Still inside the centre circle, Pearce receives the ball back and with one touch – *one touch* – he lays it forward with his right foot – *right foot* – to Bannister. Time to stop? He's already brought the ball forward and left Carl Tiler in charge of a very creaky defence. Sod that. Someone has to drag this team – nay, his club – out of the mess in which it finds itself. So he keeps running – somehow lifting those mechanical thighs in a fluent and graceful manner of which a rebooted Terminator could only dream.

Bannister has it. He faffs about a bit. Then Pearce runs past him. The thought of ceding possession is not an option. Not now. Pearce is now about to break beyond the final line of defence. Your left-back is now breaking through the lines in the 83rd minute and demands the ball be returned to him. Like any sensible human being, Bannister does the right thing.

Pearce bends his run and remains onside but Bannister's ball has forced him wide a little – left of goal. Tony Coton does what he's been told to do since he was around ten years old and hurtles out to narrow the angle. A touch to compose oneself in such a situation would be entirely understandable but Pearce doesn't need one. He only needed one touch earlier in the move so why more than one now? He slides the ball under Coton with the aplomb of Dennis Bergkamp. An away point is secured.

From back to front in 20 seconds with the ball not once coming away from the deck and helped along its way by some one-touch football. This is everything that Clough loved – this goal has his signature writ large in neon light on it.

But perhaps more significantly, the driving force was a lumberjack of a left-back who supposedly was capable of only one thing: whacking diminutive right-wingers into and over the advertising hoardings or whacking a dead ball into the corner of the goal. Just general whacking really. Need something whacked? Pearce was your man.

See, that's the thing. Forest fans had known for years that Pearce was a footballer: one who dragged them out of the mire and had played this move an incalculable number of times both on the training pitch and competitively. The only surprise here is that it was Bannister and not Nigel Clough who held the ball while Pearce bombed forward. Pearce into Webb/Clough/Gemmill – out to Carr/Crosby/Parker/Woan – back to Webb/Clough/Gemmill – into Pearce – strike on target. This was no trade secret on the part of Forest; this was simply what they did from around 1986 to 1993.

As the ball found its resting place in the City net, Pearce strode over to the away support in celebration. But he was mobbed by his grateful team-mates – they surrounded him, got in front of him and unwittingly impeded his progress towards his quarry.

But not for long. Like empty cans tied to the back of a newly wed couple's car, Clough, Bannister, et al were left behind in his wake. He wanted to share the moment with the fans. His arms were clenched by his side and his head upright with that expression on his face.

You know the one, the one that screams, 'I am utterly blessed to be doing what I do and while I am doing it, I will strive with every atom of my body to do you proud and when I do a good thing, I will be the proudest person that ever did live. Look upon my works and despair.'

A foreshadow of his Spain moment four years later.

Of course, Pearce scored a bucketload of jaw-droppingly decent goals: his Exocet missile of a free kick into the Stretford End goal in 1990 while a bunch of jeering Mancunians bated him by vocally asking him who missed in Italy was what modern parlance and vernacular might well express as a magnificently executed burn.

Forest fans had adored him for so long that when the Spain thing happened, they didn't disown him or decry others for finally realising his magnificence. They simply sat back in satisfaction that they had seen and enjoyed this for so long.

Besides, they still knew something that most had yet to learn –
what a stunning footballer he was.

The goal at Maine Road wasn't particularly meaningful or
historical – Forest ultimately finished bottom of the pile and
were relegated. Pearce scored more meaningful goals than this
and certainly more spectacular ones.

But this goal showcased Pearce at his very best: determination,
skill and beauty.

Stan Collymore
vs Peterborough United
(1994)

I N a Nottingham city centre pub, Stanley Victor Collymore leads the throng in a chorus of 'You've Lost That Loving Feeling'. It's 2017 and his love for the club hasn't diminished; it might even be stronger now than when he was banging in goals from left, right, centre and impossible angles between September 1993 and May 1995.

Given the traumatic denouement of the 1992/93 season – relegation and Brian Clough's retirement – it should have come as no surprise to anyone with a sliver of grey matter to see Forest's start to the subsequent campaign resemble two elderly removal men heave a grand piano up a narrow stairwell to a loft conversion.

A mere 45 seconds into the season and already, the piano was slipping. In fact, Forest were about to experience one of their lowest points of the 90s – certainly in terms of league position anyway. Roots Hall, the home of Southend United, was the venue as they kicked off their first season outside the top flight since Brian Clough had taken them up in 1977.

This was a new experience for many and if truth be told, it kind of seemed like it might be fun: new grounds, win some games, sashay lickety split back up to the Premier League where it was all kicking off fitter, happier, more productive and generally eating better. Most of the old gang was still there: Stuart Pearce, Ian Woan, Steve Stone, Scot Gemmill...it was all going to be fine.

But it wasn't. They were still punch-drunk and in a state of trauma at the rug, floor and solid mooring that was Clough being torn away from under their feet. They just didn't realise it quite yet.

In the early 1960s, one in five television sets purchased in Britain were made by ECKO in Southend, which seems apt since the television cameras were there on this Sunday game to gawp at Forest's fall from grace.

Barely a minute after kick-off and Pearce was in the referee's notebook for a clumsy challenge. This was to be expected though; this was fine. It was just a case of Psycho laying down a marker and explaining to anyone watching that he wasn't going to take this Football League thing lightly. In fact, it was nice to get a good old-fashioned reducer in early doors.

Just 30 seconds later and the piano clattered to the floor with a bit of a bang. Brett Angell capitalised on some truly comedic defending to put the Shrimpers a goal to the good. Shards of black and white keys lay strewn around the floor.

Hang on...what was that? What happened there? Oh. It was only Mark Crossley lying concussed and bleeding profusely. That piano is never ever getting put back together.

As if it could possibly get any worse, a glance at the Forest line-up that day confirmed that it did indeed contain Lee Glover and Robert Rosario. Now since Brian clearly had a soft spot for Glover, this wasn't disastrous but Nigel Clough was no longer around to provide intelligent movement and deft touches. Instead, Rosario was lumbering in a five-yard circumference around the edge of the penalty area, just looking at birds in the sky or thinking about the best way to avoid the traffic to get home.

Despite looking physically imposing, Rosario – so the story goes – once yelped in pain and almost turned on the water works while receiving some stitches in his head for a minor cut while representing the club. Yet here he was – expected to play his part in digging his team out of a sizeable hole by doing something he had been finding exceptionally difficult – score goals.

Things weren't going well. It wasn't meant to be like this. Could Forest get a do-over? Start again?

Somehow, Forest fought back to claim a point thanks to a Pearce penalty and were, in the end, unlucky not to take all three. It got a bit hairy there for a minute but once they got going, all would be well.

Except it really didn't get going until November, by which time, Frank Clark's team sank down to the depths of the division – such depths that to Forest fans were previously very much unexplored.

Next up after Southend were Derby County and once again, Forest were staring down the barrel after Michael Forsyth stopped laughing at Crossley's John McEnroe headband just long enough to put his team ahead. Luckily for Forest, Ian Woan equalised with an Ian Woan goal – you know the one: delightful touch, turns to find space, lashes one in. Nonetheless, this wasn't really panning out how it should have done, how everyone thought it would.

A 5-3 win at home against Grimsby Town provided Forest with their first notch on the goalpost but from there, they spluttered, coughed and wheezed through August. A win at Luton Town was sandwiched by defeats to eventual champions Crystal Palace and Barnsley. A particularly shambolic home defeat to Stoke City and a ridiculously in-form Mark Stein followed but there was one sliver of silver to be had: David Phillips bagged a goal on his home debut, converting a cross from Stan Collymore. Something was stirring.

'I missed the first few months with a virus that gave me an ulcerated mouth,' explains Collymore in his autobiography, *Tackling My Demons*. 'I shed about two stone in weight with that virus.'

By the time of a tricky-looking tie in the League Cup at Wrexham, the virus was subsiding. Phillips hung up a cross from the right and Collymore nodded in. He was off the mark. Not satisfied with that, he promptly claimed his second and third goals – the latter being a neat foreshadow of things to come. He latched on to a through ball and before he even had a touch, the ball was destined for the net. Oddly enough, this turned out to be Collymore's only hat-trick for Forest; he specialised in braces, scoring seven during his time. Nonetheless, a titanic collapse allowed Wrexham to bag two in a minute as they earned a 3-3 draw.

Then came Bolton Wanderers away and although Forest lost – again – Collymore was settling in. His first strike here was another classic Collymore goal, receiving the ball with his back to goal before executing a Kenny Dalglish-esque turn of speed and slamming the ball hard into the net. It wasn't much different from his third at Wrexham but this time, he had a defender to beat and a harder starting position.

Phillips crashed in a second goal from somewhere around Horwich to put Forest two ahead but once again, in spite of another Stan goal, they somehow contrived to lose 4-3. This was the fourth defeat of the season under Clark and the month was still September. And yet, Collymore's ability to conjure a goal from thin air offered hope.

Before it could get better though, it got slightly worse. A home shellacking at the hands of Millwall meant that by the end of October, Forest were 16th in the table. Salvation was very close though and rather improbably, came atop a windy hill in Birmingham.

'The turning point came when we played Birmingham at St Andrew's,' says Collymore. 'Lars Bohinen made his debut in that game and he made a massive difference.'

Glover scored a brace and naturally enough, Stan himself troubled the scoresheet. Such an occurrence was becoming a habit as from here on, Forest would only lose five more games all season.

By November, Collymore was unstoppable, bagging seven goals alone in that month and helping his team go unbeaten for three months.

The Birmingham resurrection was the first in a bizarre run of four consecutive away games. Next up were Wolves where

Collymore claimed his fourth goal in three games in a 1-1 draw. This was memorable for a hugely satisfying audible clunk as his finish nestled in the net after taking out the boom microphone nestled there.

For Collymore, there was an extra dimension to this goal, 'I was particularly pumped up for the game against Wolves at Molineux because Graham Turner, the man who let me go when I was banging in goals for their reserves, was still in charge. I scored a great goal that day, threading the ball between their last two defenders, taking it one-on-one with their keeper and slotting it past him. I went over to Turner in an angry celebration just to let him know what I thought of his decision to offload me.'

While you're on Cromer pier, you might as well fish for crabs and Forest made a clean sweep of the West Midlands with a 2-0 win at West Bromwich Albion – both goals scored by Collymore. As he burst through from the halfway line before dispatching his second of the afternoon, the boos from the home end were audible. Clearly, such disapproval was borne of Collymore's roots – hailing from up the road at Cannock in addition to his association with Wolves as a reserve player – but no doubt there was more than a tinge of fear in there as he simply ripped the Albion defence to shreds without even pausing to pop the discards into the waste paper bin.

Collymore had found his mojo, hit his groove and warmed to his theme all at once. The last of these away day specials was a trip to Sunderland and with the game finely balanced at 2-2 with 13 minutes remaining, Collymore decided that the game needed to be won. It mattered not a jot that Forest were deep within their own half; when he decided such things, they must happen.

Des Lyttle held the ball above his head preparing to take a throw-in near his own corner flag. Collymore came down the line and nodded infield to Bohinen who dinked it back to him as he hugged the touchline, still comfortably inside his own half. Collymore ran. He crossed the halfway line, cut inside and larruped one in from outside the area. This was just what he did and for the sixth time in those four consecutive away games he netted, helping earn ten points from that period.

'Sometimes the boys would punt a ball up to me and I would turn and run at someone and score. I'm not being arrogant. Watch a video of that season. That's the way it was,' he said.

It's true too. That pretty much sums up the way things were.

It was on a blazing hot April day in Cambridgeshire that the dual trauma of Clough's exit and second-tier football was exorcised.

Collymore himself sees his winner in a 3-2 victory as his most sentimental goal. Two goals down after seven minutes, Forest stormed back thanks to Collymore scoring twice and fittingly, a Stuart Pearce header to secure promotion. Collymore's winner was somehow both typical and improbable, 'I hit a left-foot cross-shot into the roof of the net at Peterborough and sparked a pitch invasion of joyful Forest fans.'

It was a special day, one for spilling on to the pitch in glorious catharsis. A day to grab whoever was nearest to you on the terrace and hug them until their ribs cracked. A day to simply marvel at the nonchalance with which Collymore once again ran beyond the defence and lashed in an unstoppable shot.

It was the best of times but even better times were around the corner.

Promotion to the Premier League kind of came and went for this team really as it and he simply cracked on with playing exceedingly good football and racking up exceedingly good results. An opening-day win at Ipswich Town (Portman Road once again cropping up at important times in the modern history of Nottingham Forest) was secured thanks to new signing Bryan Roy. Up next were champions Manchester United at the City Ground. Could Collymore do it against the big boys?

Absolutely.

'Inevitably, I scored. I always scored against United. Almost always. I picked the ball up midway inside their half and touched it past Incey [Paul Ince] who was tempted to go through me but rather uncharacteristically backed off. I took it on and shot from about 25 yards and it beat [Peter] Schmeichel at his near post. I thought that if I had scored against the champions I could score against anybody,' he said.

Collymore only went and did it again in December too but this time at Old Trafford, helping to secure a famous win. Pearce played a crisp ball forward to the feet of Brian Roy who in turn found Collymore. As the red shirts of United converged on him, Collymore unleashed a blistering left-foot shot that found the corner of the goal. Old Trafford went eerily quiet in disbelief; they had, after all, just witnessed the first concession of a home goal that season.

The season culminated in a defining third place for Forest. Only a wretched November and February kept them out of reach of the title, which Blackburn Rovers claimed, inspired by Alan Shearer in his pomp.

For Collymore, 50 goals in 78 games meant that his card was marked, 'Forest were offering me £12,000 a week to stay, which at the time would probably have put me second only to Alan Shearer among the best-paid players in the Premier League, and Frank Clark was hassling me to sign it. But I had my heart set on a move.'

And so, after the tantrums, the isolated celebrations, the rejection of the celebrations of his team-mates and more memorably, the scarcely believable goals, Collymore joined Liverpool, leaving Forest to embark upon their European adventure without him, effectively taking a pay cut to do so: 'My wages had gone up to £10,000 a week.'

Collymore joined a club on its knees, writhing around on the cold, hard floor. He didn't do it alone but he did play a significant part in helping the club shake off its self-pity and elevating it to its highest standing since Clough was at the helm. They were fun times while they lasted and were over all too soon.

Paul McGregor vs
Olympique Lyonnais (1995)

P AUL McGregor spent his career as a footballer
challenging the lazy stereotype. Thrust into the national
spotlight after scoring the goal that nudged Forest into the
quarter-finals of the UEFA Cup and in doing so, ensuring they
were the only English team remaining competing in Europe, he
was a prolific goalscorer at youth and reserve team level.

It wasn't easy breaking into an outstanding side that finished
third in the Premier League and made a successful foray into
Europe the year after. McGregor had to be patient, 'I was always
a centre-forward. I'd scored 49 goals in 51 games for Forest's
youth team. That's what I did – I scored goals. But then I looked
at Forest's first team: Stan Collymore, Bryan Roy...but they really
rated me and Frank Clark was of the opinion that he had to get
me in the team.'

After Collymore's departure to Liverpool, chances to prove
his worth presented themselves. Hailing from Liverpool made
a performance at Anfield all the more sweet, 'We went 2-0 up at
Anfield in Collymore's first game against us since leaving. We
battered them in the first half. I think I played the best half of my
life. I tore them to shreds. Mind you, I came out for the second
half and within 15 minutes, I had full-on cramp. I was playing
against the Kop as a Liverpool fan and it was incredible – one of
the greatest moments of my life.' Despite taking the lead, Forest
lost 4-2, consolidating their dreadful record at Anfield.

Another moment that he is rightly proud of is scoring a goal
that was voted European goal of the month at Hillsborough

against Sheffield Wednesday in a 3-1 victory. Stephen Howe opened the scoring with a stunning volley but McGregor was not to be outdone.

As the ball pinballed around in the penalty area, he rose to execute a stunning overhead scissor kick that saw the ball sail into the top corner of the Wednesday net. The man bamboozled by McGregor's acrobatic prowess that day was not Kevin Pressman but defender Steve Nicol. It matters not though – not even Peter Shilton would have saved it.

It would be in the first leg against Olympique Lyonnais at the City Ground when McGregor's star would dramatically rise. The first round of the UEFA Cup served Forest with a sentimental tie against Malmö FF, reminding many a fan of that balmy evening in Munich. The second round produced a much sterner test against French champions AJ Auxerre. A Steve Stone goal was the marginal difference between the two sides over two legs. Olympique Lyonnais would be no pushover with Florian Maurice and Ludovic Giuly spearheading their attack.

The game was deadlocked. On 72 minutes, Frank Clark took a gamble and withdrew Bryan Roy and Andrea Silenzi for Howe and McGregor. The impact was instant. Ten minutes later, Scot Gemmill hoisted one over the defence for McGregor to chase and the panic in the Lyon defence was palpable. Goalkeeper Pascal Olmeta and defender Jean-Christophe Devaux both jumped for the ball and got themselves in a right old tizz. The ball dropped on the edge of the box for Howe to volley goalwards. Olmeta was on the floor and helpless yet Florent Laville did the keeper's job by sticking out his hand and intercepting Howe's shot. Red card. Penalty.

Stuart Pearce steps up. His shot is low and hard but too close to the keeper. He parries it to the edge of the six-yard area. McGregor is alert, beating three Lyon defenders to the rebound. He finds the far corner and mayhem ensues. He runs towards the crowd punching the air. He's spotted some of his mates in the Lower Bridgford and is loving every second before he's mobbed by his team-mates.

Well, all apart from Colin Cooper, who in his desperation to get to McGregor has ended up smashing into the goalpost after the Lyon keeper sticks out an arm.

After the bitter exit against RSC Anderlecht in the 1983/84 UEFA Cup, Nottingham Forest are back in love with European football.

⚽ ⚽ ⚽

Despite this, and a goal in the next home game against Manchester United, McGregor's first-team chances remained sporadic. Relegation was around the corner after a disastrous 1996/97 season. In came Dave Bassett and Pierre van Hooijdonk and the stay in the First Division was brief. Yet after the sale of Kevin Campbell and Colin Cooper, van Hooijdonk did his thing and the outlook was very bleak – relegation was a very distinct possibility.

In came Ron Atkinson and McGregor's face simply didn't fit, 'I was delighted because he'd done a big thing in *Match* magazine a few months before about the best young players in the UK. There were six of us and I was one of them. So, he just walked on the training ground and I thought "brilliant, Dave Bassett's gone".

'I respect Dave Bassett by the way, he was completely honest and said, "I'm bringing in these types of people; they're probably not Forest types of people but we're going to get promoted," which they did and he did do a job. Atkinson walked on and he went, "Right, let's see what we've got here," and out of youth team, reserve team, first team, he went, "I don't want any fucking rock stars in my team." You just sink. The blood drained out of me. I absolutely sunk. I mean, how to cut the legs from a footballer. So I asked to go on loan.'

This meant leaving Nottingham and the club that had nurtured him from a young boy to a man. What made it even tougher to take was that this came directly after he had fought his way back from injury and back into the first team squad.

But it wasn't the end. In fact, a loan move to Carlisle United, struggling in the third tier, initially provided him with a much needed confidence boost, even though he was, at first, a little circumspect: 'I went into the digs there and it was a bit of a culture slap for a young Premier League footballer who'd done Europe and all that kind of stuff. It was stinky curtains and proper seventies décor. I walked into the dressing room and it was a completely different story.

'I've got a full Paul Weller hairstyle and "Modded" up to the max and the big centre-half was there and he looked at me and suggested that I needed to go and sit with him – Scott Paterson [at the time, seriously rocking the Mod look] and I was all right from then on. We talked about The Small Faces, Weller and Northern Soul.

'They were just a great bunch of lads. Forest had completely changed – the ethos had changed and it was back to what felt like my era. It was good camaraderie and I was the first name on the team sheet.'

From the northernmost reaches of England, McGregor found himself packing his bags and heading for Plymouth Argyle after a brief loan spell at Preston North End. It was in the south-west that he enjoyed a resurgence. First though, there was the business of negotiating the dark waters of leaving one club permanently for another, 'Michael Knighton [then Carlisle chairman] tried to sign me permanently. A most bizarre moment: he sat the big end of the boardroom – really big table as you can imagine – and he hadn't put any of the lights on. It was really dark.

'"Right. We want to sign you. I know what you are earning right now but we can't afford that so you'll have to take a drop," he said.

The offer though was short of what McGregor had been earning as a youth at Forest. 'But he did it like this: He wrote it on a piece of paper, folded it up and slid it down the table towards me like a Bond villain. So, I'm trying to check for his third nipple and I had to walk down to the end of the table and take it off him. I looked at it and thought, "That's not going to happen." But then Plymouth just pursued me like mad. They really made me feel special. Chris Hargreaves was there; we were a couple of long-hairs.'

It was at Plymouth where McGregor's goalscoring ability was let out without a leash, bagging 19 times in 77 appearances.

Eventually though, the boots got hung up and the guitar got picked up, 'If I want to do something, I'll go and do it. I just don't see any barriers.' Retirement from the game was simply a new chapter in his life, 'I got offered a contract by Grimsby: some other provincial seaside hell-hole and I thought, why the fuck do I want to go and live in Grimsby? I was single at the time and 28; my band's name [Ulterior] had just been put of the cover of the *NME* so the reason I retired was the band got good. I just thought, I'm 28 and I've had 11 years at this and I was looking at...I'd had a tough time coming from such great stock under Clough from playing the game properly.'

Slightly saddened but certainly not daunted by the thought of not lacing up his football boots again, he was keenly aware of the gaping hole that such a move can create in a footballer's life, 'Football is perpetual youth; the same as being in a band and when it all stops, stuff comes crashing down on you that you've not had to consider. You go from getting good money for essentially doing stuff you did on the playground. You don't even have to think about things beyond the game really and then suddenly, it's gone. And you're grasping and you're falling and you're Alice down the hole, grasping at anything you possibly can, be they drugs or alcohol.'

While at Forest, he had fronted the extraordinarily short-lived indie band Merc and played Nottingham's Rock City, but that was never anything serious. Ulterior though would rev into life and assault the music landscape. They played London's Astoria alongside The Horrors and These New Puritans. They looked around and saw Peaches Geldof, Douglas Hart and Bobby Gillespie.

McGregor said, 'I came out of football and thought that if we were going to do this, we were going to do this properly. It wasn't pretend – we went at it and gave it everything – full on at 200mph. We were this beautiful bubble of nihilism. We'd play a pub and it would be like Suicide on crack with Mary Chain feedback; none of us moving, head to toe leather just standing there as if to say, "We don't care, you're having this."'

But in some ways, they were victims of their own hard forged reputation. Offers were made from record companies but were rejected out of hand. Indeed, such was their perceived nastiness that other bands were strongly advised to stay away from those nasty Ulterior boys or risk losing their own recording contract.

Nonetheless, being asked to support The Sisters Of Mercy on their extensive 'Merchandised' European tour of 2009 indicates that beyond the mess of eye liner, spray paint and general rock-and-roll demeanour, there was a good deal of substance beyond the style.

Of course, in typical Ulterior style, the tour was not without its initial problems, prompted by bassist Karl Januskevicius almost bringing the whole thing crashing down. McGregor explained, 'Karl bailed out hours before the tour, "Mate, I can't do the tour. Mate, I'm not feeling it. I don't feel like it's right for the band."'

The phone went down, words were exchanged and urgent phone calls were made. Bass lines were learned on the tour bus while travelling through the Alps and all went swimmingly.

Premier League footballer, rock star and managed by Brian Clough. McGregor has packed a lot into his life. Naturally, he recalls Clough with reverence. After his youth team won the league and cup, McGregor recalls, 'He walked with us and we got a standing ovation. He stood us in the centre circle and he gave every single one of us a big hug and a big kiss and he was crying. He was so proud of us and you felt it. If you took a bollocking, you took a bollocking but you felt loved too. Other clubs didn't have that, didn't have this icon. It felt special at the time. He was such a presence.'

All the great Clough stories leave the participants and the reader with a sense of genuine wonder and McGregor's is no different, 'We were playing against Derby for the youth team. My dad always used to stand on the right-hand side. Derby broke down the wing and the ball came into the box. I think we were drawing 1-1 in the semi-final of the Midlands Cup.

'The ball came down the left wing and was bouncing around at the edge of the box. We were scrambling around trying to get it in.

'The next thing I hear is Cloughie bellowing at me "BLONDIE! STAND STILL." I'm not sure what to do. I'm still trying to reach for the ball but again I hear him loud and clear, "FUCKING STAND STILL." So I stop and stand bolt upright, because you did it. At this point, my dad chirps up, "What you doin' lad?"

'Brian Clough's screaming at me. My dad's screaming at me. Do this. Do that. So I'm stood still, in a bit of a huff. The ball got cleared and went down our right-hand side and into our box yet I'm still stood where I was told to on the edge of their box. Everyone's laughing. Around 2,000 people congregated around the touchline, all laughing.

'They hit the post and then our left-winger surged forward and I became onside again. He crossed the ball and I'm thinking, "It's coming, it's going to land right for me," and it did. I struck it right in the top corner. Cloughie came running down the touchline, "ARCHIE! I FUCKING TOLD HIM!" in joyous celebration.

'Talk me through that? I'm not into any otherworldly superstitious bollocks but how do you logically explain that?'

You can't though can you? Genius is very difficult to unpack and dissect.

Frank Clark, Brian Clough and Nottingham Forest left a deep mark on McGregor, 'When Clough was there, he stood for something.

'Frank Clark stood for the same things. For a long time, Nottingham Forest were everybody's favourite club, everybody had respect for Forest, for the way they played.

'If you said you were a Nottingham Forest supporter, it stood for something: it meant a certain moral structure, a certain moral DNA, you stood for what was right. It was almost like saying, "I'm a socialist. I'm one of the good people in the world. I support a team that tries to play football the right way and I call out cheats."

'As a player, you felt that and you represented Nottingham Forest Football Club. Forest stood for something. If you supported them, that's who you were. That's what this club stands for, and is.'

Ian Woan vs Tottenham Hotspur (1996)

T HE mention of Ian Woan's name does strange things to Forest fans born between 1980 and 1988.

Fully-grown and bearded men tend to go all misty-eyed before wondering aloud at length how Jason Wilcox and Steve Guppy managed to acquire four England caps between them yet Woan remained overlooked. Anger tends to be expressed, followed by resignation before settling for the fact that they will always have their very own 'Ian Woan' moments.

Should a person of this demographic ever encounter Woan in the living, breathing flesh, they grow very emotional, proclaiming to his face that when they were a kid, he was their absolute and total hero.

Despite the sentiment being honest, such moments can be a little awkward to witness. Yet it is easy to understand why the affable scouser retains a very special place in the hearts of Forest fans coming of age to the soundtrack of Oasis, Blur and Pulp. Straddling the entirety of the 1990s in Garibaldi red, Woan scored very special goals.

In time-honoured fashion, all of this very nearly did not come to pass. While whipping balls around for fun at Runcorn, Woan caught the eye of Harry Redknapp, then in charge at Bournemouth.

He even went as far as shaking Redknapp's hand on a deal to sign for the Cherries, 'I only signed pro at 22. I had been working as a quantity surveyor and playing for Runcorn. I was supposed to be signing for Bournemouth.'

Intriguingly, Woan had already caught the eye of future Forest manager Frank Clark when he was in charge at Leyton Orient. Clark so very nearly signed Woan before Clough's intervention.

'Then two days before I was due to go there was a phone call,' he told NFFCTube. 'I met Ronnie Fenton and Alan Hill at Northwich Victoria's ground, and I was a Forest player before Brian Clough had even clapped eyes on me. I think they must have been looking for a left-sided player and read about me in the paper.'

He got his dad to phone Harry to tell him the deal was off.

'But I have the highest regard for Brian Clough. He took a chance on me without even seeing me play. I owe him everything,' Woan said.

Woan walked in to a club with a League Cup on the mantelpiece and a third-place finish under their belts. In addition, Stuart Pearce sat growling in the corner while Des Walker zipped around the place at lightning speed with composure and élan. The boy from Runcorn was understandably a little overwhelmed at first.

Ten months later, Woan made his debut at Carrow Road in a 6-2 demolition of Norwich City. This was all rather fitting since Woan's father, Alan, played for Northampton Town and Crystal Palace yet started his career at Norwich. Poignantly, he made his own Football League debut at Carrow Road at 21 years old – the same as his son.

In typical Clough fashion, Woan was only told on the day that he was on the bench. After playing for the closing 20 minutes, young Woan scoured around for a pay phone to inform old Woan that he had just appeared in Clough's first team. The journey began.

For the next few years, things ran quite smoothly. Forest finished in eighth place in Woan's debut season and reached the FA Cup Final but, unsurprisingly, his memories of that day are rather miserable. He saw at first hand Paul Gascoigne out of control in the tunnel and despite a first-half lead and a penalty save by Mark Crossley from Gary Lineker, it was not to be for the men in red.

Still, two years previously, Woan was playing in the West Cheshire league so things were going relatively well from a personal perspective.

His fine goal in a 2-1 win against Liverpool that May extinguished any lingering hopes that the Merseysiders had of retaining the title ahead of Arsenal. With the score at 1-1 and Liverpool desperately chasing a much-needed win, Woan nonchalantly (he seems to have done an awful lot of things nonchalantly on the football pitch) chested the ball and picked his spot before firing into the roof of the net. Since then Liverpool have yet to win a title: that is the closest they would come.

Oddly enough, Woan repeated this title-denying behaviour almost exactly five years later with a stunning equaliser against Kevin Keegan's Newcastle United in a 1-1 draw, again at the City Ground, again in front of the Trent End. If you need a title party pooper, Woan is your man.

The following season – 1991/92 – saw another eighth place in the league secured along with another League Cup Final, this time a defeat to Manchester United in an acrimonious and somewhat tedious game. Then it all fell apart.

'The relegation season of 1992/93 had a disjointed feel to it,' says Woan. 'It was not a happy camp.'

Yet Woan stuck around to play a significant part in not only returning Forest to the top division but also taking it by storm. The period that he calls 'the highlight of my career' was about to achieve lift-off.

Frank Clark replaced Clough and achieved promotion, a third place finish in the Premier League and European football. Woan, like pretty much everyone else on the planet, really warmed to Clark, 'He was a great man-manager, a really good guy and a good coach. We had our ups and downs but he played me and we had a good dialogue. I really enjoyed working with Frank Clark.'

Europe beckoned in 1995 and fittingly, Forest were pitted against Malmö FF in the first round of the UEFA Cup. The Swedes had been their opponents in the final of the European Cup in 1979. Some might say you couldn't write it but you could certainly pull it out of a velvet bag.

It was Woan who set the memorable European journey going with his opening goal in Malmö following a pulsating run by Steve Stone, who centred for Bryan Roy to feed Woan close in but wide left. He squeezed the ball in at the near post. Forest would get a bit of a pummelling for the rest of the game and were slightly fortunate to come away with only a 2-1 deficit.

While flying back, Woan was in deep thought. He enjoyed this. He wanted more of this. But at 2-1 down, there was a real risk there would be no more nights like this. A sense of frustration overcame him: 46 games for this?! For one two-legged tie?! No. Surely there should and must be more.

There was. In the return leg, Roy crashed one in from the edge of the Trent End penalty area and further ties against AJ Auxerre, Olympique Lyonnais and FC Bayern Munich followed.

It was during this season that Woan scored one of his iconic goals. In another of those serendipitous Woan moments, Tottenham Hotspur were the visitors to the City Ground for a fifth round FA Cup tie at the back end of February. The game should have been played a week earlier but was abandoned due to the most memorable of snowstorms in Nottingham that rendered a usually five-minute walk to the nearest McDonald's into something akin to an Antarctic trek.

A week later, the snow was gone and the game went ahead. In the time it takes for the average length of a pop song to play out, Forest were awarded a free kick on the edge of the penalty area. Stuart Pearce wasn't on the pitch that evening but Ian Walker – in the Spurs goal – could not rest easy since Woan, Colin Cooper and David Phillips were all in deep conversation about who would get to strike it.

All had pedigree in the 'lashing free kicks home from 25 yards' stakes. On this occasion though, it was Woan who made

Walker look foolish to give the Reds the lead after three and a half minutes.

Chris Armstrong reduced the early lead to rubble by scoring twice before half-time before Woan scored the most improbable of goals. It all stemmed from Ronnie Rosenthal wrestling the bullish Stone to the ground as he cut in from the right in front of the Main Stand A block.

❂ ❂ ❂

A free kick is awarded right on the line of the penalty area – but not the horizontal line, the vertical line. And it's 12 yards out from the touchline. While up from the back lumber Colin Cooper and Steve Chettle in an effort to get on the end of it, this signals to Walker in goal that he should focus his attention on them and not the shot. Consequently, he organises (in the loosest sense of the word) only a two-man wall.

For all their qualities, Cooper and Chettle aren't blessed with height and so Woan thinks again…could it? Might there be space to…?

Sod it. Might as well.

So he does. He does indeed fancy having a pop from there and the ball arrows straight into the top corner. Two arms aloft, he struts towards the A block, nodding appreciatively at his own handiwork, something he later said of, 'I've tried it a million times on the training ground and it's ended up in the Trent.' It's an outrageous goal – reeking of bravado and hubris.

❂ ❂ ❂

But this was the mid-90s when anyone could do anything; the possibilities were endless. Want to form an era-defining rock and roll band and end up quaffing champagne with the prime minister? No worries.

Fancy smacking in an unstoppable shot from an acute angle that rattles the stanchion of the goal? Feel free.

It was a time of baggy, swagger and oversize Premier League shirts and this goal was the epitome of that narcissistic era. If Paul Gascoigne's goal against Scotland under a scorching midsummer Wembley sun at Euro 96 was the definitive 90s summer goal, Woan's was the winter equivalent.

The replay was won at White Hart Lane owing to a magnificent contribution from Mark Crossley in a penalty shoot-out after a 1-1 draw. After saving Teddy Sheringham's penalty and securing a passage to the quarter-final, Crossley ran the length of the field in celebration before belly-splashing on to the wet turf in boyish delight.

The fun ended there though as Aston Villa inflicted a humbling defeat at the City Ground thanks to a goal from – of all people – former Red Franz Carr.

It was a pleasing season for Woan as he ended up Forest's top scorer with 12 goals – outscoring Bryan Roy and Kevin Campbell. Yet there was disappointment on the international front as Steve McManaman got the nod ahead of Woan for a friendly against Bulgaria in March as preparation for the forthcoming Euro 96 tournament to be held in England.

A little under a year later, Woan was at it again – 'it' being banging in outrageously good goals from improbable distances. An FA Cup tie against Kenny Dalglish's high-flying and as yet undefeated at home Newcastle United at St James' Park was, on paper, very difficult. In reality, it was even harder once Les Ferdinand nodded Newcastle into the lead. Yet in a rare foray forward, Woan tried his luck with a daisy-cutter from distance and after a slight deflection, Forest were on level terms.

It was Woan's first goal in 25 matches but that isn't important right now: what was important was the seal was broken, the top was off and the cat was very much out of the bag. Confidence started to ooze through his veins.

Moments later, Warren Barton, under pressure from Roy, produced the most bizarre defensive clearance in hoofing the ball up in the air in the very loose direction of 'away'. It bounced around the corner of the penalty area as Woan closed in. He chested it – like he did against Liverpool six years previously – and found himself around 12 yards out, like against Spurs the year before, but this time he was just inside the area. The ball bounced up once more before being ferociously leathered into the top corner.

It was just as outrageous as the one against Spurs and perhaps even more enjoyable since this was against a very good team from a very poor team that was hurtling headlong towards relegation.

Things were once again falling apart. The squad had become stale as key sales started to bite. Players like Jason Lee, Steve Blatherwick and Andrea Silenzi weren't quite up to the high standards of the previous years and Clark was unable to arrest the slide. Dave Bassett came in.

As for Woan, chronic tendinitis developed in his right knee as a result of using his left peg so often. This curtailed his training and his fitness suffered. It was a slow rehabilitation and in hindsight, Woan admits he should have stepped back and got the knee sorted rather than trying to play.

After Bassett came David Platt, signalling the end of Woan's Forest career. The Platt era left a 'sour taste in my mouth. We didn't get on.' He was substituted against Stockport County on the final day of the season in a 3-2 win where, despite a packed away end, the football was poor. Once back in Nottingham, he walked off the bus, drove home and it suddenly dawned on him: that was it. He would never play for the club again.

Ten years at Forest ended not with a bang but with a whimper. He remains a little bitter, perhaps angry, that there was no opportunity to say thank you to the fans or to have a testimonial. Platt wouldn't allow that. 'We fell out early,' Woan explains. 'My first-born was just born and I was late for training so we fell out. "Not committed to the cause." We just didn't get on.'

No contract talks. No testimonial. No thank you. No goodbyes.

After brief stints at Barnsley and Swindon Town, he left for America to join Columbus Crew yet was traded to Miami Fusion with no consultation. He returned to England and enjoyed a last hurrah with Shrewsbury Town, making a healthy 50 appearances and scoring seven goals before one final crack at America with the wonderfully named Syracuse Salty Dogs ahead of coaching Burnley under the guidance of another former Forest employee, Sean Dyche.

While he left Forest under something of a cloud, his feelings for the club remain unblemished, 'When I think about Forest, it's always with a smile on my face. To be a small part of 150 years of such a football club is special to me.'

Steve Chettle vs
FC Bayern Munich (1996)

'*RE di Roma*' proclaimed one flag, held aloft amid a sea of crimson red at the Stadio Olimpico on 28 May 2017. They came in their thousands to honour a man who made 786 appearances for his club over a period of 25 years – a boyhood fan born in the city.

In the modern world of football, such stories rarely happen. The notion of a kid standing on the terraces cheering on his heroes, and later training and playing professionally with those he idolised as a youngster, is heartwarming enough. Throw in the fact that he would end up third in a table of most appearances for the club and we're beyond cockles being warmed stuff and well into Roy of the Rovers territory.

Just like Francesco Totti, Steve Chettle proudly served his hometown club.

As a kid, he would be hoisted upon his dad's shoulders in the old Trent End to get a better glimpse of his heroes John Robertson and Ian Bowyer conquering England and then Europe. It wouldn't be too long before he was striding out for the first team, having been sent on by Brian Clough.

Imagine that – watching your football club lift some industrial amounts of silverware as a kid and then going on to play with them. For real. Just for good measure, chuck in the fact that Clough happened to be your boss and you start to get a handle on the Steve Chettle story.

Most people's brains would have climbed out of their heads in sheer disbelief at the thought of such events actually happening.

Not Chettle though. Not much fazed him. Even less got past him. He spent his career unruffled. No fuss required.

Clough had a tried and tested strategy for giving young lads their debuts and Chettle's was a textbook case. 'I wasn't told hours in advance – it was two o'clock by the time that the message came and it was nerve-racking. I was surrounded by seasoned, serious professional footballers, and players like Webb, Pearce and Walker,' he told Nottingham Forest periodical, *Bandy and Shinty*. Chettle debuted against Chelsea and then started playing at right-back when Gary Fleming picked up an injury – all before his 19th birthday.

As usual, Clough knew exactly what to say in order to get the best from his charges. 'I was playing out of position at right-back but the great man just told me "to go and play right-back like a centre-half which is what you are",' said Chettle. 'He kept things very simple – you knew your roles and responsibilities. My role in the team was to head it, kick it and, if possible, keep it and give it to somebody better than me in the team – which he told me was everyone at the time.'

They are words of advice that frequently crop up when a footballer speaks about life under Clough.

Chettle developed from there, working alongside Paul Hart and Des Walker before making himself a permanent fixture at the heart of the defence. The principles instilled in him served him well as Clough's gang of nice young men spent the 1980s playing nice football, maintaining nice haircuts and being polite to referees.

That's not all though as towards the tail-end of the decade, they twice picked up silverware in the form of the League Cup. Chettle was on the bench for the 1989 win against Luton Town and alongside Walker and his mate Stuart Pearce for the successful retention of the trophy a year later against Oldham Athletic.

Hot on their heels came the disappointment of the FA Cup defeat to Tottenham Hotspur, 'It passed me by a little bit, the whole occasion. I'd take it in more looking back if I had a chance and another go at it but you were utterly consumed by the FA Cup Final. We started the game really well and if Gazza [Gascoigne] had stayed on the pitch we probably would have won the game. In the end we fell a bit short and couldn't lift the trophy.'

Lurking around the corner was relegation and the end of the Clough era. Yet all was not lost. Frank Clark took the helm and steered the ship back to third in the top flight and into Europe as they reached the quarter-finals of the UEFA Cup. The side fizzed with pace, talent and metal and at the heart of it all was, according to Clough, 'A local youngster totally committed to the club.'

Chettle relished playing with such talent in the shape of Bryan Roy, Colin Cooper, Ian Woan, Steve Stone and naturally, Stuart Pearce. Ploughing a lone furrow up front was Stan Collymore, 'a genius with the football. The English version of the original Ronaldo – he was strong and quick and had everything.'

Having watched his team face down and defeat Europe's best, Chettle was doing it for himself now, walking in the footsteps of those he idolised as a kid, 'We were unfancied – we were this little Nottingham Forest team. We had to try to keep as many clean sheets as we can. We went to Auxerre and Stoney [Steve Stone] nicked a goal, we kept a clean sheet and it was a really good time – we were a great unit. Those memories of Europe will last forever.'

He didn't score many but there is something poignant about the goal for which he is most fondly remembered. Pitched against FC Bayern Munich for a place in the semi-finals, Forest travelled to the Olympiastadion for the first leg – the very place where 17 years earlier, they lifted the first of their two successive European Cups.

⚽ ⚽ ⚽

With the home team ahead thanks to an expertly taken header by Jürgen Klinsmann on the quarter-hour mark, Forest win a free kick a minute later wide on the left.

Pearce places the ball with the demeanour of a seriously pissed-off man.

He walks away as if he's ready to fight the oxygen surrounding him. Maybe the full force of the awfulness of the yellow wasp-vomit shirt he is wearing has just hit him. If that wasn't enough to push a man to Hulk-like levels of anger, he's sporting yellow shorts and socks too. All-yellow kit with some wasp vomit besmirching his chest and the awfulness has just hit him on a freezing evening in Bavaria. No wonder really.

Overcome by his ire, Pearce needs a moment alone so David Phillips casually jogs up to swing one in with his right foot. It sails over everyone. Oliver Kahn is already thinking about the resulting goal kick. Then Chettle pops up from nowhere and casual as you like, simply nods it in. Manager Frank Clark had done his homework, identifying that the German team were, on occasions, a little casual in defending the far post.

It takes a full second for everyone to digest what has happened. There is a stunned silence. Did he...? Has he...? Is it...? HE HAS! IT IS!

Chettle is away towards the corner flag. Stone pursues him with a look of disbelief etched across his loveable large face. He can't believe it and neither can Chettle if truth be told. He even points to himself as if to tell his team-mates that yeah, that was him. Drink it in, lads – drink it all the way in.

⚽ ⚽ ⚽

'People ask what my most memorable goal was, thinking of that, but the thing I will always remember is looking like the most surprised man in the world after scoring – I was supposed to square it back across the goal but the ball was spinning too much and Oliver Kahn [Germany international goalkeeper] just waved it by,' says Chettle.

The same stadium as one of the club's defining moments. The same goalposts into which Trevor Francis scored a goal that defined his career. Heck, just to cap it all off, it's even a similar type of header. All that is missing is a tumble and roll on the discus circle.

He continues, 'I was very privileged. I still live in the city and people still talk to me now about it. It was amazing, the stadium and that game reflects high on everybody's memories of Forest and to score in the same goal as the great Trevor Francis in the stadium that Forest won the European Cup was absolutely amazing. Not too many people remember the home leg but I prefer it that way!'

The home leg went less well. Forest left Germany with a promising 2-1 defeat but Munich steamrollered them 5-1 in the return. Then again, Munich boasted not only Klinsmann and Kahn but also Lothar Matthäus, Mehmet Scholl, Christian Ziege, Andreas Herzog and Jean-Pierre Papin. They went on to crush FC Girondins de Bordeaux in the two-legged final 5-1 after edging out Barcelona in the semi-final. Not a bad team really.

Chettle eventually left the club in 1999 having spent 15 years there. He might not have shared the skills of Totti but not many players enjoy a long and fruitful career with the club they supported as a boy and supported from the terraces.

Imagine telling the young Chettle on his dad's shoulders that he would go on to make more appearances for the club than John Robertson and Stuart Pearce, that he would not only play with Ian Bowyer but make almost as many appearances as him, that he would get to go to Europe and follow in the actual footsteps of the European Cup-winning team, that he would be a mainstay of two vibrant, exciting sides – one under Clough and the other under Clark, Clough's favourite left-back. Imagine that.

'I'm very proud of what I achieved and when I look back on it now I know I was successful and very fortunate to be in two teams that achieved good things,' he says.

He should be proud since Nottingham Forest is proud to have been served by Steve Chettle for so long.

Chris Bart-Williams
vs Reading (1998)

A RE the good times worth the bad that follow? Is the high of a debauched weekend in Ibiza diminished by the comedown of a return to moving boxes around a cavernous warehouse for a living come Monday morning? Is the two-pint sweet spot destroyed by the rest of the evening spent copiously vomiting in a dingy gig venue toilet?

The mind likes to sift through the wreckage and cast the dull stuff aside like flotsam and jetsam into a sea of discarded memories for the sharks to have their way. This is, generally speaking, a very good thing.

Us humans are after all merely ill-conceived vessels inherent with more design flaws than the spire atop the Church of St Mary and All Saints in Chesterfield which happens to house a bunch of vital organs yet in spite of all this, the ability to sift out the actual journey to Manchester to see Forest chuck beer all over City's FA Cup experience in January 2009 is something to be cherished and celebrated.

All that time spent queuing up, all those glasses of tap water, all those bang-average support bands you've experienced fall by the wayside of that thrilling ride, that perfect pint on a hot day and your favourite band walking on stage and kicking off with something from their back catalogue that most around you haven't heard but you know intimately, to which you smugly mouth along.

When Chris Bart-Williams swivelled like an eel on a helter-skelter and banged the ball into the Reading net beyond Scott

Howie, elation, nirvana and bliss were achieved. Forest were back in the big time having achieved promotion as champions only a year after being ushered out of the back door of the Premier League like an uninvited guest showing up at a party clutching a bottle of Diamond Blush yet heading straight for the unopened bottle of Dom Perignon.

All was well with the world again. Yet what the earth giveth, it taketh away in double...and then some.

If Forest fans knew then that Bart-Williams's goal would lead only to a season even more disastrous, embarrassing and miserable than the previous relegation season, would they savour the elation? Would they jump out of their seats and hug strangers all over again like they did on that sunny April day in 1998 when the Bartman found the net?

Of course, promotions aren't composed of a single strike. Throughout the season, Forest were an unstoppable goalscoring machine, obliterating opposition defences as if they were harmless alien invaders in a 1980s arcade game under Dave Bassett. Yes, that's right – Dave Bassett.

Featuring Kevin Campbell and everyone's favourite kid who goes home with his ball if he can't be on the winning side, Pierre van Hooijdonk, the very worst it got for Forest during the season was a three-game run in September in which they picked up only a point. Even Ian Moore bagged a goal that season.

Hardly a nadir.

The stats are mightily impressive: eight defeats, 28 wins, 82 goals scored, goal difference of +40 and Manchester City relegated. There was a League Cup exit at the hands of Walsall but that's palatable since it was Walsall and some things in life are pre-destined and not to be tampered with. Some things in life simply *are*. Forest losing to Walsall is one of those things.

At the end of it all was Chris Bart-Williams. It was he who clinched promotion and the title with a late winner against a desperate Reading in the dying embers of the game.

Signed from Sheffield Wednesday in the summer of 1995 on the same day as Campbell, Bart-Williams was in some ways tasked to step into the boots of the departed Lars Bohinen. Officially speaking, Stan Collymore left for Liverpool on the very same day too.

It took the Forest faithful a while to work out exactly what Bart-Williams was. He wasn't blessed with pace and seemed ponderous in possession; not quick enough or possessing an engine for midfield and too timid in the tackle for centre-back. Only when Paul Hart shunted him to something approximating an old-fashioned sweeper role did he really show his class. In 2000/01, he pillaged 16 goals and ended up top-scoring in an otherwise entirely forgettable season in which the fixture list culminated in Forest facing Stockport County, Wimbledon, Gillingham and Tranmere Rovers, having scraped through a hard-fought two-legged League Cup tie against Darlington.

From a vantage point of 2018, one could be forgiven for thinking that Nottingham Forest had inexplicably slipped into the Conference for a season.

Bart-Williams was a slow burner. He made 33 appearances in the UEFA Cup season of 1995/96 yet like everyone else around him, he struggled in the subsequent campaign as Frank Clark was asked to clear out his desk when Forest floundered to the very bottom of the table. Back to the First Division it was then and with no Stuart Pearce to drag them up by their collective bootstraps. Instead, Dave Bassett was at the helm.

Despite the frankly ridiculous goalscoring exploits of van Hooijdonk with 34 from 45 games, Middlesbrough and Sunderland pushed Forest hard throughout the season even though both were comprehensively beaten at the City Ground, 4-0 and 3-0 respectively.

Going into the penultimate game against bottom club but 'in with a shout of survival' Reading, a win would secure promotion. As expected, it was a tense affair, especially the first half in which neither team could muster up the confidence to string a couple of passes together – both partially paralysed by nerves. Any flashes of goal were fleeting for Forest as Linvoy Primus marshalled the away defence superbly.

Sensing the home side's nerves, it was Reading who started to chance their arm in the second half. Paul Brayson slammed a shot beyond the despairing dive of Dave Beasant only for the ball to rebound off the post. It wasn't just squeaky bum time; it was full-on freak-out panic stations at DEFCON 1.

☻☻☻

As the game barrels towards a stalemate, man of granite Colin Cooper hoists a free kick from the centre circle towards...well, anyone really. Somehow, it evades everyone and drops on the knee of Bartman. It looks like its going to bounce away from him but he quickly resolves this with a second touch. The problem though is that his back is to goal and no one – not a single one – is making any effort to move for a lay-off. Paralysed by nerves, see?

There is no other option. He's going to have to sail this ship alone.

In the blink of an eye, he's shimmied to the side and left the Reading defender to grab a hot dog. Only six yards out and one on one with the goalkeeper. The angle is narrow though; he's on the corner of the six-yard box. Little option but to slam it hard, slam it true and hope for either a rebound for the lurking van Hooijdonk or close your eyes and hope it finds the top corner of the near post.

Before Howie has a chance to even think about setting himself, the ball whizzes past him into the far corner – low and hard and true.

It's not necessarily joy that is released in that very moment the net ripples. It's something more akin to raw, primeval and unconfined relief. Forest are back.

☻☻☻

It was glorious while it lasted but that summer, soundtracked by 'Brimful of Asha' and Run-DMC Vs Jason Nevins, held a tinge of sadness as before August rolled around, Campbell was sold to Trabzonspor and then Cooper to Middlesbrough. And then Pierre took his ball with him.

It all fell apart as quickly as it was put together and 12 months later, Forest stared up from the bottom of the Premier League table with a mere 30 points, relegated with three games to go under the leadership of Ron Atkinson who could barely find his way to the correct dugout, never mind scrap his way out of a relegation battle.

And then to top it all off, enter David Platt.

That debauched weekend in Ibizia? That two-pint sweet spot? Forget about it. Gone. Blown away in a breeze of financial mismanagement at the hands of Hurricane David. It would get a lot worse before it would get any better. The millennium bug did actually strike; just not in the way everyone expected. It turned out to be a localised phenomenon – confined to West Bridgford – causing nausea, anxiety, apathy and a strange feeling akin to wandering around the doldrums for a few years while wearing boots made from treacle.

There was precious little to shout about from the moment the ball left Bart-Williams's foot. They were beautiful; they were doomed.

Nonetheless, once Forest allowed him to sit back and mop up the mess ahead of him, they realised what a talent Bart-Williams was. Particularly delightful was watching him step forward to size up a free kick on the edge of the opposition box: he hit the spot more times than an acne-ridden teenager applying antibiotic cream to their face.

He seemed a quiet, mysterious type too – the kind of player who might sit you down, make you a cup of tea and give you a hug were he to catch you looking a bit glum on a Monday morning. In an interview with *The Guardian* in 2001, he proclaimed that 'women crying' made him feel depressed, his mum to be the living person he most admired, his fantasy to be the first black president of the US, his motto to be 'always wear a good pair of shoes', to believe in life after death since 'I believe in Casper the friendly ghost,' and the rather heartwarming stance that life is 'really all about love, isn't it?'

After leaving in 2002 for Charlton Athletic he had spells with Ipswich Town, APOEL in Cyprus and Marsaxlokk in Malta, followed by a stint coaching in America.

He should know that he is remembered fondly where the mist rolls in and is welcome back any time, good pair of shoes or not.

Andy Reid vs
Sheffield United (2000)

L ATE November 2000. The millennium bug saga had passed and the clocks still worked. More importantly, Andy Reid made his debut for Nottingham Forest and scored with a beautifully taken goal to secure a 2-0 win against Sheffield United at the City Ground after Ben Olsen had opened the scoring.

After some teething problems, Paul Hart's young team matured from giddy little pups to young adolescence. The 2002/03 season was a vintage one as Hart's vibrant group reached the First Division play-offs. Reid was outstanding on the left side of midfield with Riccardo Scimeca, Gareth Williams and David Prutton completing the almost entirely home-grown engine room of this dynamic side. In addition, Michael Dawson, Marlon Harewood, John Thompson and Craig Westcarr also progressed through the ranks, all steadily calmed by Des Walker at the back.

Reid certainly enjoyed playing in this team and learned a lot from the avuncular leadership of Hart. He explained to the *Irish Examiner,* 'He always wanted us to try and play football, to play out from the back.

'I always remember him saying to us, "If we play this way, we are going to give the ball away. But I'll never give out to you about it – as long as you switch on straight away and give everything you've got to get it back."

'Paul Hart was brilliant and I don't think anyone could have got a better football education, not just technically or as regards positional sense but in terms of football etiquette as well – how to conduct yourself on and off the pitch.'

Indeed, the development of Reid not only as a footballer but also as a man was forged around this time. After all, Reid had left home in Ireland at the age of 17 in an effort to fulfil his potential as a professional footballer in England. Furthermore, to do so would mean leaving behind his baby daughter. Nonetheless, Reid flourished under Hart's leadership.

It was Reid who gave the team its creativity. He rarely beat the opposition right-back for pace – he wasn't that type of winger. Hart utilised a midfield diamond, allowing Reid the licence to drift in behind the front two and not only pull the strings from there but skilfully craft and bend the strings to his will with that left foot of his that was so highly educated and cultured that it could give Stephen Hawking a run for his money. The football played by this team lives long in the memory.

Reid himself looks upon his early days at Forest with fondness. 'The season we got to the play-offs, when Paul Hart was manager, was a fantastic season,' he told *Left Lion*. 'We had a great team on and off the pitch. It was a really enjoyable time and we played some great football. It's just a shame we couldn't go all the way and get promoted. It was disappointing that we couldn't capitalise on the good work and bring in some more players. In fact, we ended up losing a few and never really replaced them.'

Indeed, it all unravelled on a hectic evening at Bramall Lane in which Forest marginally ended up on the wrong side of an epic play-off semi-final against Sheffield United. If only the team could have held on to the lead given to them by Reid in the 57th minute after he surged forward to latch on to the end of a Matthieu Louis-Jean cross to hammer the ball home and in doing so, give his team a two-goal advantage. It is also worth remembering the sumptuous pass by Reid that put David Johnson through on goal to lash Forest into the lead in the first leg at the City Ground.

As debt and mismanagement crept up on Nottingham Forest, he and Michael Dawson were sold to Tottenham Hotspur in

February 2005 for £8m. He enjoyed some highs but struggled to hold down a place in the side. From Spurs, he joined Charlton Athletic where he got back into the groove, receiving plaudits and love from the Addicks fans and left them with a more than respectable scoring record of eight goals in 38 appearances. From there, he rocked up at Sunderland and despite some impressive displays, found himself loaned out to Sheffield United and eventually sold to Blackpool. His seaside sojourn was brief though and on 1 July 2011, he came back home to Nottingham.

His re-signing offered the club hope. Not only was he a throwback and a reminder of a successful period in the club's history, he slotted snugly back in and displayed admirable leadership qualities over the course of the season in which the wheels well and truly fell off as Forest struggled to recover from Steve McClaren's unsuccessful tenure and later the tragic loss of Nigel Doughty. Reid cajoled, harassed, harangued and dragged what was required from the team to survive relegation.

Indeed, Reid mark II was a different animal to the youngster that left the club. His game had adapted and he was comfortable sitting deep in midfield and perhaps surprised everyone with his mobility in making challenges and protecting his defence. He was also the fulcrum of the team's attacking intent and the sight of him with the ball at his feet in the opposition half, looking, turning, looking, twisting and ultimately delivering a ball as he orchestrated the play was a common and pleasing one.

There were goals too: stunning ones. In October 2003, Reid collected the ball in the wide left position around the halfway line at Upton Park and ran forwards before smacking it into the top corner. In goal for West Ham United that day was David James, who remembers the strike well. 'Long-range shot. That was annoying!' he told Nottingham Forest periodical *Bandy and Shinty*. 'You should never get beat from that far out. It was just, "Oh, he's shooting, and oh, it's in!" I do remember it. Top-left, sort of top-leftish.'

Just to prove this wasn't a fluke, Reid repeated the same trick nine years later at Peterborough, doing pretty much the same

thing. Reid's unerring accuracy in shooting at times made the art of walloping a ball into the parts of the goal that keepers cannot reach look very simple and natural. Against Blackburn in 2014, he casually walloped the ball from range into the top corner with the absolute bare minimum of backlift, before the goalkeeper could even adjust his feet.

The first is always special though. Against Sheffield United, Reid latched on to the end of a David Prutton pass and bore down on the Trent End goal on 63 minutes. He calmly slotted in to secure a 2-0 win – Forest's sixth in seven – after Ben Olsen opened the scoring. After banging goals in for fun at youth and reserve team level, Reid was up and running in the first team.

Another impressive aspect of Reid is the manner in which he conducted himself. Often on the end of derogatory chants about his weight, the lifting of his shirt to reveal his stomach or the cupping of his ears was never an option for him. He didn't get angry – he just got on with the game, which usually involved swinging in a dangerous cross after trotting over to the corner quadrant, allowing opposition supporters to direct their taunts directly at him.

There's always been another side to Reid the footballer too. He seems like a normal and interesting person in whose company a pint or two would be accompanied by an engaging conversation. 'The main reason why I like people like Che Guevara and James Connolly is because it can't have been easy for them to go to a different country and try to liberate people from a different country,' he explains. 'People can fight for their own country because it is their own country. But to go and help other people from outside their country. To help them be free because they believe everybody should be free is a massive thing.'

That damp and chilly Wednesday years ago in November 2000 was the starting point for a wonderful career and Reid's return to his spiritual home in which he played some of the best football of his career was a privilege to witness.

Andy Reid – a History Boy who came home.

Julian Bennett vs Yeovil Town (2008)

A WALK over Trent Bridge from the city centre is dominated by the picturesque vision of the City Ground sitting snugly by the banks of the Trent. Few divert their eyes right, which is a shame since the beautiful Wilford Suspension Bridge, reminiscent of the Brooklyn Bridge in design, strides majestically across the water. Traverse one way over the bridge and you will find yourself in leafy West Bridgford: a highly desirable postcode boasting Trent Bridge cricket ground, coffee shops and boutique bars. Go the other way though and you enter The Meadows: a very different place, certainly if reputations are anything to go by.

As a boy, Julian Bennett must have strode over the Trent from The Meadows, bound for the City Ground's Centre of Excellence, with a head full of hopes and dreams: to play for the first team, to know the feeling of wearing the red shirt with the tree emblazoned on his left chest, to lead the team out and perhaps ultimately, to score a decisive goal. It would take time and a few disappointments along the way but he would one day know how all of this would feel.

Bennett is one of many Nottingham-born players who would go on to play for Forest, including Viv Anderson, Steve Hodge, Steve Chettle, Darren Huckerby, Jermaine Jenas, Wes Morgan, David McGoldrick and Lewis McGugan. In varying degrees, all found a place in the hearts of Forest fans – local players are deservedly afforded that extra patience and support that might be denied outsider journeymen.

But on 3 May 2008, Bennett slammed in a goal that would not only epitomise his playing style but also get Forest moving forward again after the ignominy of being the first European Cup winners to fall below their domestic top two tiers and restore some pride in the club.

It was a long and arduous journey in reaching this moment though. Bennett left the Forest Centre of Excellence at 14 in 1996 only to pitch up at Walsall eight years later. It was at the Bescot Stadium that his career gathered pace, making 51 appearances for the Saddlers between 2004 and 2006.

In the space of two days in January 2006, Walsall lost two players who would go on to further their careers elsewhere: Matty Fryatt left the Bescot Stadium on 9 January to play for Leicester City and a day later, Bennett booked a train ticket to Nottingham. It was an easy decision for him to return home, 'Lots of other teams, including ones in the Championship, were showing interest in me, but this is my home-town club and it's a dream come true.'

There was no lingering resentment towards the club for how it ended in Nottingham eight years ago – just pride in staying true to his path and his upbringing. 'I had played for Forest up until I was 14. It did not work out,' Bennett told the *Nottingham Evening Post*. 'I could easily have gone out there to do bad things, but I knew I didn't want to disappoint my parents. My dad drummed into me that I needed to finish school. I was into computers. I wanted to get a job in that and I got nine A to Cs [GCSEs].'

He was under no illusions about playing for the once champions of Europe under a certain Mr Brian Clough and Peter Taylor. But champions of Europe, Nottingham Forest were no longer. Indeed, the club was struggling to come to terms with being a relatively big fish in the über Darwinian slugfest that is League One.

But he was fully aware of what was required of him and the club. 'In the Cloughie days the club was at the top of English football, and myself and the fans, we want to be back up there competing with the best teams in the world,' he told *The Guardian*. But there was the little case of getting out of the third tier of English football to contend with first.

It all came down to a teeth-grindingly exciting afternoon of the final day of the season on a scorching day in May 2008. After the trauma suffered at the hands of Yeovil Town in the play-offs a year earlier, Forest had to beat the Glovers and hope that Cheltenham Town could pull a result out of the hat against fellow promotion-chasers Doncaster Rovers down at Whaddon Road.

Tension gripped the City Ground. The situation required someone to stand up and be counted, to lead from the front, to metaphorically grab their crotch and bellow, 'This is our time. Let's not mess it up.' In the 12th minute, Bennett did exactly that.

⚽ ⚽ ⚽

As Kris Commons hoists a ball up to Grant Holt in the hope he will hold it up on his copper-barrelled chest, Bennett makes his way upfield, loitering with intent on the left side. Holt is thwarted in his efforts and the ball is cleared to the Yeovil right-back area. Terrell Forbes looks like he should deal with this and set Yeovil off on a counter-attack.

He doesn't get the chance though as while Forbes is looking for an outlet, a juggernaut comes thundering into him from nowhere, leaving him prone on the ground. There's no question of a free kick though – the Forest left-back indisputably wins the ball. Play goes on as the ball cannons into Nathan Tyson but he can't hold the ball up and the defender nicks it away from him, sending it back in the direction of Bennett.

Unbelievably, Bennett is up and on his feet again. He collects the ball but he is comfortably outside the penalty area and more importantly, he is moving towards goal from the left and being predominantly left-footed, there seems little risk of Bennett being able to create an angle for a piledriver of a shot.

No matter though. The boy from The Meadows adjusts his body after skipping around the floored Forbes and smacks the ball with the outside of his left boot, beyond the despairing arm of Steve Mildenhall. It is the perfect combination of craft, dexterity, skill and sheer brute force determination. It is exactly the type of goal a certain Stuart Pearce would have scored from a similar spot on a similar occasion. Compliments in and around the Nottingham area don't come much bigger than this.

Colin Fray nails the radio commentary, 'Julian Bennett – Forest's Player of the Year, the lad born just down the road in The Meadows, wins a thumping tackle and then thumps the ball into the net and gives first blood to Forest on what could turn out to be promotion day.'

⚽ ⚽ ⚽

It did indeed turn out to be promotion day as the dice rolled at Whaddon Road went in favour of Forest and a remarkable series of events conspired to allow the club automatic promotion to the Championship, gatecrashing second spot in the table at exactly the right time despite barely troubling the top two places throughout the entire season.

Forest ran out 3-2 winners thanks to goals from another Nottingham lad, Lewis McGugan, and nearby Mansfield-born Kris Commons. Furthermore, Bennett played a key part in the promotion effort, helping his side to 24 clean sheets – a season's best for the division – and making the PFA's League One Team of the Year. Not quite champions of Europe but back on the road to recovery, thanks in large part to the boy from The Meadows.

Nigel Doughty, who sadly passed away almost four years later, was all too aware of the hurt of the previous three seasons, 'This has been my club since I was five or six and I have felt embarrassed that we have dropped into the third tier. I will still be a bit embarrassed until we are back in the Premier League because this is a Premier League club. We should be established at that level and pushing on to achieve things from there.'

Everything was in place and all was set for a new era of respectability in the Championship for the club.

But football has the habit of tweaking your nose and flicking your forehead just when you think you've got everything in its rightful place. The following season, Forest endured a torrid start under Colin Calderwood, reaching an absolute nadir on Boxing Day 2008 with a a 4-2 defeat to Doncaster Rovers at the City Ground that cost Calderwood his job. As if that wasn't bad enough, Bennett damaged his cruciate and cartilage ligaments in that game, ruling him out for the rest of the season.

The club did rally under the guidance of Billy Davies and not only avoided relegation but went on to establish themselves as a team to be reckoned with under the fiery Scot's leadership, regularly gate-crashing the play-offs. Bennett himself never quite recovered though.

Loan spells at Crystal Palace and Shrewsbury Town and transfers to Sheffield Wednesday and Southend United followed his spell at Forest but over four years, the Nottingham-born lad made a measly total of 38 appearances. Eventually, Bennett was all played out and a series of tweets confirmed his retirement.

Football, like life, doesn't always reward the good guys. Having to retire due to injury robs a footballer of his trade and for Bennett, this was a cruel and prolonged affair. But then again, scoring such an important goal in the history of your boyhood club is surely the stuff of which dreams are made and the boy from The Meadows can retire safe in the knowledge that he played a huge role in dragging the club back from the wilderness.

For that season and that moment, Julian Bennett created a little bit of history.

Dexter Blackstock vs Bristol City (2009)

POP music is littered with hit singles that are utterly unrepresentative of the band or artist's usual output.

But all of this raises an age-old philosophical question: is it worth taking the Faustian road travelled by Robert Johnson and sell your soul to the devil in exchange for uncanny musical talent and subsequent success?

When Terrorvision dropped their annoyingly catchy hit, 'Tequila', in 1998, it was against the wishes and votes of their fans who had been canvassed via the official fan club and wanted 'Day After Day' to be released. But when Zoe Ball gave 'Tequila' traction on Radio 1, the nation's public was treated to an endless procession of Tony from Terrorvision grinning into the camera with his endearing gap-toothed grin.

The very next year, their record company dropped Terrorvision after their follow-up single 'Ill Wishes' reached only number 42. Talk about wind being knocked out of sails. Similarly, The Ramones enjoyed a huge hit on both sides of the Atlantic with their cover of 'Baby I Love You' by The Ronettes in 1980. Rarely has there been such a defining example of juxtaposition than when those leather-clad mop-topped boys lazily strummed along to one of their biggest chart smashes in the UK by a country mile. The buzzsaw guitars of 'Blitzkrieg Pop' never felt so far away.

Rightly or wrongly, these bands are likely to be remembered for songs that seem at odds with their *oeuvre*. This is not to say that there is anything offensive, disappointing or substandard when it comes to the songs under discussion; just to say that both bands have an extensive back catalogue which, were one to explore solely on the basis of 'Tequila' or 'Baby I Love You', one might be somewhat surprised and, truth be told, a little disappointed.

Dexter Blackstock was not a Ramone and neither was he a founding member of the Keighley-based Terrorvision. He is though rather fondly remembered for a goal that – come the shakedown – pretty much staved off the threat of relegation back into League One in 2009 after only a season back in the Championship. Like The Ramones and Terrorvision though, his defining moment is not entirely representative of his back catalogue.

The significance of this goal should not be understated. While relations with close members of your family were strained beyond tolerance and you were swigging from a bottle of cheap sherry on Boxing Day 2008, Colin Calderwood was having an even worse festive season than you. His Forest team endured that horrifying defeat at home to Doncaster Rovers who were at the time managed by, of all people, Sean O'Driscoll. Forest were slip-sliding away down a slippery slope.

Dignified and sound as he was – and having finally dragged Nottingham Forest (somewhat fortuitously) out of League One after three years down there – Calderwood was finding the going somewhere between granite-like and rock solid. His time was up. Merry Christmas Mr Calderwood.

John Pemberton was given a long brown overcoat and a big bunch of keys to accompany his role as caretaker manager. Things changed for the better. Fellow strugglers Norwich City were dispatched at Carrow Road and implausibly, moneybags Manchester City were humiliated on their own patch in the FA Cup in a game featuring a rather wondrous Nathan Tyson goal and at the other end of the spectrum, City's rather surreal pre-game parading of new signing Wayne Bridge. After that, Billy Davies took ownership of the long brown coat and big bunch of keys.

Like the sweet whiff of a brand new car though, this upturn was fleeting and transient. After a five-game winning streak which lifted the club to the dizzy heights of 17th in the table, there then followed its polar opposite: five defeats on the bounce. Slip-sliding again.

A couple of wins brought brief respite. But then another five games without a win, including a 5-0 shellacking at Turf Moor, played out.

Six games left. Twenty-second in the table. League One standing there beckoning the club with its wrinkly and gnarled pointy finger, enticing it with a slightly easier life, where things weren't so bad, where it might actually win a game of football once in a while.

But the fans remembered: they weren't to be fooled. They weren't falling for that crock of lies and deceit again. League One was horrible and they really didn't want to be there again.

Billy Davies rolled his sleeves up. Billy Davies wasn't going to go silently into the night. Billy Davies was about to embark upon some serious speaking about Billy Davies in the third person action and drafted in a bunch of loan players over the international break. In came Chris Gunter, Isaiah Osborne, Iain Turner and on 26 March – after a limp 1-0 defeat at home to Wolves (who won the league) – in came Dexter Blackstock.

It is worth dwelling on the bizarre circumstances surrounding Blackstock's signing from QPR: a club that was undergoing its own existential crisis. Under the ownership of Flavio Briatore and Gianni Paladini, manager Paulo Sousa was under fire. Bizarrely, this turbulent time in QPR's history was documented on film in the feature *QPR: The Four Year Plan*.

The moment when Blackstock's loan deal to Forest is finalised is there for posterity and is recalled by QPR blogger Loftforwords, 'Later, in an equally extraordinary scene, Briatore and Paladini, angry at then manager Paulo Sousa's refusal to play two strikers in games, have decided that striker Dexter Blackstock should go on loan to Nottingham Forest. Blackstock, QPR's top scorer at the time, is seen sitting at a table with a Forest contract in front of him shaking his head while other people in the room urge him "don't sign it Dext, you don't want to go". Paladini, laughing and smiling, tells him it's a good move for him and he should go and get some games. Suddenly, randomly, Fitz Hall arrives in the room demanding to know what's happening and asking, "Why are we loaning our top scorer out? Don't we want to make the play-offs?"'

QPR's loss was Forest's gain. Slowly but steadily, the gales and biting winds blowing the good ship Forest off course eased. A point was earned at Oakwell after the international break.

Still in 22nd place – below the perforated line – not enough, but a start. Five games left.

Draws were encouraging but wins were required. Up next was a very respectable Bristol City side at the City Ground.

Ivan Sproule put the visitors ahead after ghosting in at the far post to somehow knock in one of the scruffiest goals you'll ever have the dubious pleasure of watching. The finger of League One hovered over the City Ground like a big National Lottery icon.

Robert Earnshaw brought parity after being played through by Blackstock. Thanks to some comical defending straight out of the drawer marked 'Chuckle Brothers sketch', the game was locked at 1-1 at half-time.

A point. A single solitary point. It's not enough.

Away trips to Sheffield United and Blackpool loomed into view – difficult places to visit.

Need to win. Don't make me go back to Gillingham or Oldham. Don't make me go back to League One.

⚽⚽⚽

Twelve minutes left. Oblivion happens. Dele Adebola scores for City after some far from convincing goalkeeping from Iain Turner (who would play only three games) – just like the big striker had done four years previously for Coventry City to slam the biggest nail you've ever seen into Forest's Championship coffin.

As the ball trickled into the net, Turner was on the edge of his penalty area. Three Forest players had their hands on their head. Kelvin Wilson chastised and berated the floor in a thinly disguised gesture of what he would like to do to his on-loan goalkeeper. Adebola had done it again. When Manchester United were relegated in 1974, Denis Law famously back-heeled a goal for Manchester City that played a huge part in sending his former club down. Law was some player. It was no consolation to United fans but at least Law was a player from the very top bracket.

Dele bleeding Adebola.

With a simple header after an on-loan goalkeeper's rush of blood to the head.

This is how it happens.

Dele.

Adebola.

Seven minutes left. Lewis McGugan whips in a free kick from the right awarded after Jamie McAllister has needlessly received a red card for the visitors. Joe Garner stoops to conquer, nodding in at the near post.

A point is still not enough but frankly, we'll take, cuddle and serenade it all the way home.

Added time. The ball is ping-ponging around in the corner until McGugan hoists a hopeful ball into the box.

Garner heads it on…to no one in particular.

Blackstock heads it on…to no one in particular.

A City defender heads it on…rather bizarrely into the area in which Blackstock occupies. He is 14 yards out and the ball is falling to his left foot – not his strongest. Two defenders converge on him and close down the space. Between the sticks, Adriano Basso takes up a decent position.

It's going to take an ice age for Dexter to bring it down and fashion and get his shot away. Or he could take it early…first time…

This is going to end up in the upper tier of the Trent End.

Instinct. Blackstock acts while others contemplate. He volleys it with his left foot into the corner of Basso's goal, screwing in off the post.

Shirt off. Fans on pitch. Colin Fray laughs aloud at the sheer audacity, beauty and downright surprise of the whole goddam thing.

Nottingham Forest are above the dotted line and will remain there.

No. They'll do better than that. They will remain unbeaten for the season and end up in 19th position and Blackstock will bag another goal at Bloomfield Road. Southampton will be deducted ten points and everyone connected with Nottingham Forest will breathe a huge and collective sigh of deep relief.

No more Oldham away. No more Gillingham away. No welcoming of Exeter City or Stockport County to the City Ground. No more Johnstone's Paint Trophy. No more lonely nights.

⚽ ⚽ ⚽

As welcome and skilful as this significant goal was, it wasn't classic Dexter.

Blackstock specialised in towering far-post headers after a good old-fashioned bout of clambering and wrestling with an out-of-position full-back who found himself exposed under the flight of the long diag. Stick the ball into the far post towards the closing minutes of a dull and mustn't-lose away game and Dexter was your man.

It wasn't pretty – he didn't shimmy past a defender or slam one in from long range – but he would somehow stick the ball agonisingly over the line then look over towards the linesman, just to check he hadn't strayed offside or that his gentle nudge hadn't been spotted.

That was classic Dexter.

Even in the infancy of his career at Plymouth Argyle, he signalled his arrival at Home Park by doing a classic Dexter Blackstock thing. Against Rotherham United in 2005, he headed home in the 76th minute after Nick Chadwick's audacious overhead kick came back off the crossbar. It was not to be: he was offside. Not to be thwarted, Blackstock scored twice against

Forest that season for Plymouth in a defeat at the City Ground that pretty much sealed the Reds' relegation to the third tier.

Classic Dexter Blackstock.

This though. This thing against Bristol City. This was 'Tequila'. This was 'Baby I Love You'.

Naturally, a permanent contract was dangled in front of Dexter's face – the first of numerous ones offered by the club – and he signed on the dotted line.

His time at Forest was eventful. He suffered serious injury against Cardiff City in November 2010 and issued a writ against Seyi Olofinjana for the tackle, claiming the midfielder to be 'negligent'. He returned to action for Forest – and Leeds United on loan – and continued to score important far-post goals after a long diag.

He bought his physio and doctors a brand new shiny iPad for helping him overcome his career-threatening injury. In March 2014, he was given a suspended three-month ban from all footballing activities after admitting multiple breaches of betting rules with a £60,000 fine thrown into the mix too. He made 164 appearances for Forest and bagged 41 goals after signing permanently. The club released him in September 2016.

He didn't single-handedly save Forest from relegation on that glorious April Saturday. Nonetheless, the club was staring down the barrel until he swung his left foot towards a football in the penalty area in front of the Trent End.

A return to League One would have crushed the heart of the club, just one year after getting out of the infernal division. Survival was the platform for some mightily enjoyable times under Davies – on the pitch at least – as Forest made themselves a permanent fixture in the top six. He scored other memorable goals too – a winner against Newcastle and a classic towering far-post header at Elland Road in that 7-3 victory spring to mind like giddy toddlers signalling their desire for ice cream.

But he'll always be fondly remembered for his hit against Bristol City, regardless of it being unrepresentative of his usual output.

Radoslaw Majewski vs West Bromwich Albion (2010)

ONCE in a while, there is a moment when everything falls into place: a perfect moment in which the inescapable feeling that this will be the one resides – all and everything is possible. A moment that takes your breath away in its perfection that might one day be celebrated and immortalised on a t-shirt with angles, explanations and scientific formulas explaining how the rules of quantum physics were pushed to the edge in order to achieve the seemingly simple task of placing a ball in a net. The boy who came to be known as Radi was at the apex of such a moment on a flesh-creepingly cold evening in the West Midlands.

Majewski was plucked from Polonia Warsaw in the summer of 2009, initially on a season-long loan, but this was made permanent a year later. He was slight; a waif of a lad but when he was on the ball, space seemed to open up. Otherwise a joyless-looking individual, he seemed playful, alive and downright happy when he had the ball at his feet.

He announced himself in some style in August by smacking in a pristine thunderbastard against Derby County to set the Reds off on a 3-2 victory. How such a trifling specimen could produce a thing of such power concerned the majority of the crowd that day but only for a microsecond...then they went absolutely bananas in celebration.

An undoubtedly sweet moment but perhaps surpassed by the seemingly impossible conversion against promotion-chasing West Bromwich Albion later on that season.

Newcastle United and the Baggies were blazing a trail at the top of the Championship but Billy Davies's men were just about managing to stay in touch. Although West Brom had dispatched Forest in the season opener at the City Ground, it was a fortunate result and even runaway leaders Newcastle left Nottingham with nothing thanks to a coolly converted Dexter Blackstock goal. If... if Forest could take something away from The Hawthorns then maybe, just maybe, promotion was a realistic outcome.

After 18 minutes, Blackstock poked in a goal from a corner and that's how it stayed until the break. Naturally, the Baggies came out forcefully in the second half but on 53 minutes, Paul McKenna once again found himself in exactly the right position to intercept an opposition pass on the edge of his own penalty area. The ball was worked forward to Majewski but he could only carry the ball backwards so he offloaded it back to McKenna who was now urging the team forward.

McKenna though was under pressure so he hoisted it up into the night sky. It should have been easy for the West Brom defence to deal with but they seemed rattled. The ball was headed aimlessly up into the air – Guy Moussi pounced.

⚽⚽⚽

Sensing weakness, players in red shirts swarm forward. Chris Cohen busts a gut to get forward and takes the ball from Moussi. Chris Gunter also appears from nowhere on the right side on the overlap. He moves the ball on and makes headway into the penalty area. Two red shirts lurk in the box on the six-yard line but Gunter overcooks the cross – it sails despairingly beyond them towards the back post, beyond the angle of the six-yard box.

But wait. A diminutive figure lurks menacingly and is approaching the ball with pace. But the angle is tight – Marco van Basten tight. Before anyone can work out the options Majewksi faces – chest it? Head it back into the box? Let it go past him in order to build again? The ball smashes into the roof of the net.

Majewski is ecstatic. His left-foot volley almost surprises himself but that's a disservice. More likely, he's overjoyed to see such a difficult shot executed to perfection and his joy is precisely that which football occasionally produces – unconfined. His celebration is a hybrid of icons: there's the double peace sign, the one arm raised and finally the shirt over the face before the towering Blackstock bundles into him and simply knocks him over perilously close to the cleared snow at the edge of the pitch. Perfection.

⚽ ⚽ ⚽

Forest went on to secure the points thanks to an excellent Chris Cohen goal – as good a team goal as one is likely to see – running out 3-1 winners against a team containing the future City Grounders Simon Cox and Gonzalo Jara Reyes. But for now, the extraordinary unbeaten away run continued into the New Year in the front garden of strong contenders for promotion.

It wasn't to be though as Newcastle and West Brom powered away from the pack – the Baggies eventually finishing 12 points clear of third-placed Forest, who would come unstuck against an indomitable Blackpool side in the play-offs. For a moment though, when Radi's volley hit the back of the net, all was possible. Forest climbed to second in the table – above West Brom – yet remarkably, went and lost their next eight away games.

When Radi was good, he was very very good but when he was bad – well he wasn't really ever simply bad, just prone to being completely anonymous at times. His tackling was as bad as that of Paul Scholes and he couldn't win a header against Alan Wright but what he did bring to the team, beyond some spectacular moments, was ball retention around the edge of the opposition box. This meant that the team had time to get up and support him and generally make things happen.

After a hat-trick against Huddersfield Town, Majewski told the *Nottingham Evening Post*, 'In the formation we are playing in, I believe I should be in the box a lot. I scored the first goal like that.' Sadly, he lacked the consistency around which to build a team.

In the summer of 2014, he was loaned to Huddersfield Town for a year and played in their 4-0 opening-day hammering by Bournemouth, which led to the sacking of Mark Robins. He would make only eight appearances all season and he drifted out of the minds of the Forest hierarchy and supporters, culminating in his release from the club in 2015.

His goals left an indelible image on the collective consciousness and will be celebrated for years to come.

Wes Morgan vs
Notts County (2011)

ORIGINALLY a large area of unloved wetland occasionally offering a safe harbour for excess water flowing down the River Trent, The Meadows area of Nottingham has evolved substantially over the course of the 20th century.

Its early incarnation featured rows of terraced houses for those that built the railways and worked in factories. Redevelopment in the 1970s in the form of the Radburn model led to countless cul-de-sacs and dark underpasses that may or may not have been a factor in the rise of anti-social behaviour blighting the area. Big wheels keep on turning though and plans to regenerate the once bustling hub of Arkwright Street are afoot. A phoenix-esque rise from the ashes is not to be discounted.

Notts County's Meadow Lane stadium is – unsurprisingly, given its name – a goalkeeper's throw from Meadows Way, likewise Nottingham Forest's City Ground a goalkeeper's downfield punt into the mixer. It is in this area, just like Peter Taylor, that Wes Morgan was raised.

Growing up, Morgan saw things. 'As a kid, I saw it all,' he told the *Leicester Mercury*. By his own admission he 'got caught up in a few things', but thankfully for him, he 'always had the football. I saw some bad things. I have good friends who have done bad things.'

Bad things.

As a 15-year-old, County rejected Morgan. Forest swooped and picked him up after seeing him playing for Midland

Football Alliance club Dunkirk. Under Paul Hart's inclusive and encouraging strategy regarding talented youngsters, Morgan's debut for Forest came in a first round League Cup tie at Port Vale in August 2003 at the age of 19. It was a drab goalless affair yet Forest left Burslem with a ticket to the next round of the cup after a penalty shoot-out.

Fast-forward eight years almost to the day. The summer of 2011 was anything but the summer of love; it was the summer of the London riots, of burning and looting in the cities. Against this backdrop of deep civil unrest around the country, Morgan – affectionately dubbed 'The Major Oak' around these parts – would play a pivotal role in a first round cup-tie that would act as a celebration for football in the city of Nottingham.

* * * * *

On the afternoon of Tuesday 9 August 2011, about 100 teenagers – contacting each other through BBM – started gathering at the city centre Arboretum, Nottingham's oldest public park.

City centre shops near Clinton Street East and Clumber Street started closing at 3.30pm.

Riot police arrived on the Arboretum about 7pm and scattered the crowds. A breakaway group occupied the roof of the adjacent private Nottingham high school for girls and threw missiles at police.

* * * * *

Notts County manager Martin Allen wanted to march his team across Trent Bridge in and among the fans, like Jon Snow going into the Battle of the Bastards with bannermen, drummers and snarling diawolves (or maybe angry magpies). This is exactly the kind of thing Allen – you don't earn the moniker 'mad-dog' for being kind to kittens – would absolutely have done were he not advised by the local constabulary that perhaps, in all seriousness, Mr Allen, in the midst of something approximating a national emergency what with riots breaking out in numerous cities at the moment and a local derby in such a major city, this really wasn't a good idea.

Not to be kept down, Allen wheeled out County legend Charlie Palmer in front of the Bridgford End packed with Pies fans before kick-off, rendering the visual spectacle something akin to a barcode party. Unsurprisingly, the away end loved it. After all, the man waving to and applauding them bagged the winner in the last league Nottingham derby back on 12 February 1994, resulting in a 2-1 victory for the Magpies.

That day is not known to some in the city of Nottingham as Charlie Palmer Day for nothing.

With the sun beating down on Steve McClaren's exposed forehead, newly installed as manager on the red side of the Trent with a raft of shiny new signings in the process of bedding in, both teams got down to business. County fancied their chances of chalking up another Charlie Palmer Day – perhaps a Mike Edwards Day – against a team barely on first name terms with each other. Forest fancied sending Allen back along Trent Bridge with a flea in his ear.

⚽⚽⚽

At 8pm, Alan Sheehan curls in a delightfully wicked cross and get this, with his right foot. Mike Edwards bundles the ball over the line. Limbs aplenty in the away end.

8.14pm. Lewis McGugan lines up a free kick. The term 'top bins' is yet to take its place in the pantheon of terminology used by teenage boys for a football heading towards the top corner of a goal frame.

Make no mistake though; McGugan's kick is definitely top bins – a free kick so classy that it resembles Andrea Pirlo in a full-length knitted cardigan.

8.55pm. American Robbie Findlay does something he so rarely did for Forest. Rather than dangling his leg in the vague direction of a football in the blind hope that it would somehow – by sorcery or witchcraft or old magyk –end up in the opposition's net, he scored an actual goal. Amusingly, the ball itself seemed to apologetically trundle into the net – maybe in complete disbelief at being set on its way by Findlay.

9.10pm. Craig Westcarr enters the fray. At the time, Westcarr was Forest's youngest player to play for the club in a league game and the third-youngest scorer. This matters not a jot now though. He trundles on in the black and white of County with 20 minutes or so to rescue the game and gets down to jostling with his old pal Wes Morgan.

9.14pm. After a bout of head tennis in the penalty area, Westcarr plucks the ball out of the air, swivels and casually pops the ball into the bottom corner. From a County perspective, tidy. Very tidy indeed.

Craig Westcarr Day anyone?

This enthralling game leaps excitedly into extra time. No one really wants to go home or walk the streets of Nottingham or help themselves to a pair of Nike Air Max trainers from Foot Locker.

9.42pm. Karl Hawley doesn't just play a ball through to Lee Hughes, he prises the Forest defence – such as it is – wide open with the ease and dexterity of a craftsman casually carving a masterpiece. The boy Moses got nothing on Hawley at this moment. The thought of a Lee Hughes Day brings spasms of pain to those of a red persuasion. Bugger.

* * * * *

At 10pm, Canning Circus police station was set alight after fire bombs were thrown at the building by a group of around 40 people. Six officers were still inside the building when the attacks began.

* * * * *

10.07pm. (In terms of the football match, 122 minutes and 7 seconds since kick-off.) Wes Morgan ambles upfield in the hope of conjuring an equaliser.

⚽ ⚽ ⚽

He remembers the goal vividly:

'Obviously it's Notts County we're playing against, rivals from just across the river, it was a big game for all the players and fans involved. It's extra time, and in my career in the last few minutes of a game I've tended to go up and try and nick something, a header, flick-on, cause some kind of problem that might get a goal. I've gone up front, the ball's hoisted up, and I remember going for the first header, not getting a connection, and it's bounced off someone and fell in to my path.

'It's outside the box and I just thought to myself just hit it as hard as you can and make sure you hit the target to be honest! And it flew in the top corner! It was a great moment and the equaliser to take us through to penalties, which we won. It was a very important goal and a great goal at the same time.

'It's by far my best goal. I probably score a couple a season, normally headers, or tap-ins.'

In terms of the celebration, it's right up there with Marco Tardelli in 1982 and Colin Barrett in 1978.

'It was a bit of everything really: the last minute, the occasion, the goal itself, and all the emotions of it. I just felt ecstatic and I remember turning round and running, and I felt like I could run forever! I ran all the way down the side of the stand, to the family section at the end, and I remember seeing some friends in the crowd and I was pointing them out. It was amazing,' Morgan says.

'I think once it had died down, people stopped jumping on me, I'm sure Westy [Craig Westcarr] was throwing a few verbals my way. You fucking this and that... haha!'

* * * * *

An hour later (23.00), the Meadows police station was attacked by 20 men and a police car set alight outside. Groups of up to 50 people damaged cars, pubs and shops in areas including Basford, Mapperley and Radford. Bulwell and St Ann's police stations were also attacked.

The total cost of the Nottingham riots police operation was £1.2m, with 225 officers deployed during Tuesday night. In total, 131 people have been arrested on riot-related charges in the city; police are still looking to arrest about a dozen more. Almost 40 per cent of those who had appeared before the courts by mid-October were aged 10-17 – with none over 40.[1]

* * * * *

There were no reports of any arrests relating to the football match that evening.

The City of Nottingham and The Meadows area will continue to evolve and tell its stories but one suspects – and hopes – that football will remain at the heart of this particular corner of the city. After all, when it throws up moments and stories like this, it should be embraced, hugged and squeezed until it hurts.

This was a day when football – irrespective of the old cliché – won.

---

1   *The Guardian* 6.12.2011

Ben Osborn vs
Derby County (2015)

W HEN Rick Blaine tells Ilsa Lund that 'we'll always have Paris', he is harking back to their brief romance on the eve of World War II – one that was ended by the Nazi invasion of France. Here, he faces up to the fact that they are unlikely to meet again and even if they were, there are higher forces at play that would make their lives difficult. Maybe subconsciously, he believes that whatever relationship they might resurrect, it would never match the one they have both idealised in their memories.

Sometimes, life is better played out on a memory loop with all the bad and boring bits removed, leaving only the stars, moonlight and fireworks.

While Stuart Pearce's reign as Nottingham Forest manager from April 2014 to February 2015 was a brief one which started brightly only to fizzle out dramatically, it yielded one of the most cherished memories of recent years for Forest fans. The fact that the last-minute winner against Derby County was scored by a player brought up in Derby is only really a small fraction of the story.

Initially a left-back with the under-17s and then utilised wide on the left with the under-18s, Osborn got his chance to play through the middle when he stepped up to the under-21s before making his debut for the club on 29 March 2014. He played the full 90 minutes of a 1-1 away draw at Portman Road – seemingly the unofficial ground at which young Forest starlets are handed their first game with the big boys.

Since that time, Osborn has been picked repeatedly by a number of managers since Gary Brazil handed him his debut days after the club parted company with Billy Davies. Despite a bewildering number of players coming and going to the club since then, Pearce, Dougie Freedman, Paul Williams, Philippe Montanier, Mark Warburton, Brazil (on three separate occasions as caretaker) and Aitor Karanka have all found a place in their starting line-ups for Osborn.

With his endless work-rate, bravery in constantly showing for the ball and flashes of quality when assisting, one gets the impression that Brian Clough would have loved him in his team and picked him every single week.

Under Montanier, player churn was particularly high yet Osborn was the only one to play in every single game, unleashing 61 shots, second only behind Jamie Ward, whose shots generally troubled the upper tier of the Trent End. He made the most passes, provided the most assists and created the most chances for Forest in a difficult season and what's more, he did all this while being shunted around the park from left wing, defensive midfield, attacking midfield and left-back.

Although his pocket-sized stature suggests he would be perfect as a cuddly toy as part of an incentive to adopt a polar bear, he possesses a determined streak and a fiercely cultured left foot. His crucial winner against Bristol City in January 2017 ended a miserable run of form for the club but it wasn't your average goal in a 1-0 win for a team battling relegation against, at that stage, a struggling rival. It was a flash of brilliance, inviting comparisons with Matt Le Tissier at his most beguiling.

Awarded a free kick midway through the second half, Osborn, Jamie Ward and Matty Cash stood over the ball, deep in consultation. Cash gently rolled the ball back a yard to Osborn, who flicked it up and volleyed into the net. It left the City Ground crowd equal parts stunned and delirious with joy, not unlike the reaction to when Willie Carr donkey-kicked the ball up in the air for Ernie Hunt to smash home in 1970. Yet it is Osborn's goal against Derby about which celebratory songs are sung. Were it just a winner against the old rivals, that would be reason enough for the goal to go down in Forest folklore. But it was so much more than that: it was a winner in stoppage time away at the old rivals' place after trailing at half-time. But even then, much remains about why this was such a special moment and in order to understand, we need to rewind to the opening game of the season.

When Pearce strolled out of the tunnel to take his place in the dugout as Forest manager on that August afternoon in 2014, a fair amount of very grown and hardened men and women would tell you they had a little dust in their eye while gently dabbing their cheek with the back of the hands. This wasn't just another manager taking charge on the day of the football season that holds the greatest of hope for all; this was Pearce returning to lead the club he loved to something approaching a state of dignity. All was possible.

Under Pearce, Forest sailed through August and September unbeaten until October kicked in, yielding four losses from five games. But this was a bit of a blip since Forest then chalked up two excellent wins: at home to Norwich, featuring a glorious last-minute winner straight from defending a corner and a comprehensive 3-0 rout away at Wolves.

Yet it quickly transpired that it was in fact these two wins that were the blip since from then on, performances plummeted with Forest chalking up only three points from 21 available. Pearce's men travelled to Pride Park on the back of four straight defeats, including a humbling loss at Rochdale in the FA Cup.

Pearce's job was in jeopardy under the trigger-happy Fawaz Al-Hasawi. Forest's record at Pride Park was dismal and abysmal; their fans steeled themselves for a very difficult day. When Henri Lansbury headed into his own goal after only 16 minutes, there was little to suggest that this would be anything but another defeat for Pearce's team at a place where above all, he would hate to lose. After all, this was the man who famously said, 'No disrespect to Derby but I have to say I could never work for that club in any capacity. And I mean never.'

Yet something changed in the second half. 'We were in really bad form running up to the game,' Osborn told the *EFL Rivalries* programme on Sky Sports. 'Stuart Pearce gave us a memorable motivational team talk that will always stick with me.'

Derby looked nervous as Forest played with increasing belief. In the 75th minute, Osborn whipped in a free kick from wide and after some penalty area ping-pong, Britt Assombalonga stabbed home. A draw. A point. That would be acceptable. More than acceptable. That would be good. Just don't lose. Not here. Not to that lot. Not under Pearce.

⚽ ⚽ ⚽

The clock trundles towards stoppage time, then into stoppage time. A long ball falls out of the sky on to Forest defender Kelvin Wilson's head and the ball bounces around in midfield – it is all Robert Tesche can do to help it on its way out wide and into space. Osborn starts running. He has the ball under his grasp now and ahead of him is a wide-open space.

As he approaches the edge of the penalty area, four Derby players chase him down while three defenders lay ahead of him, the nearest of whom is Richard Keogh who ambles slowly towards Osborn, no doubt hoping that Osborn will lay the ball off to the closely guarded Assombalonga.

Keogh suddenly changes his approach. With a sense of urgency, he slides in to Osborn's feet since he sees his body shaping to shoot. Before Keogh hits the ground, the ball fizzes past him at lightning speed and ripples the black and white coloured netting.

One corner of Pride Park dances around in unison like a particularly violent swell. Tesche grabs Osborn in celebration with a manic grin plastered on his face. Osborn seems cool – casual even. Not because he doesn't get what he's just done but more likely, precisely because he knows just what he's done.

He has stuck the ball in the Derby net and for such moments, songs will forever be sung. In the away end, a son grabs his father and holds him close, seeking to squeeze every last single rapture from this brief period in time.

For Osborn, it all seems quite natural and normal. 'The ball dropped to me near the halfway line. I didn't realise exactly how late it was. I got around the edge of the box and struck it cleanly. Looking back, it makes the hairs stand up on the back of your neck,' he would later exclaim.

Elsewhere, the injured Andy Reid and Chris Cohen cause a bit of a stir in the posh seats but it is down on the bench where a certain Forest manager's mask of, up to now, professionalism and calm exterior has slipped right off and lays tattered on the floor.

When Pearce came back as manager, he seemed keen to shed the old 'Psycho' tag. There was a distinct absence of fist-pumping, growling and snarling. He conducted post-match interviews holding a polystyrene cup of coffee and seemed about as likely to smash heads together in the dressing room, as he was to renounce his life-long love for The Stranglers.

Not now though – he can hold back no more. There is fist-pumping, arm-raising and a look on his face that belies the months of showing only to fans Pearce the football manager. His face is thunderous with joy.

For a second or two, he is the Psycho who saluted the Trent End, the Psycho we shared with the country in the penalty shoot-out against Spain in Euro 96. Christ, how we missed him. It was damned good to see him again. Still crazy after all these years.

⚽ ⚽ ⚽

Of Osborn and his performance, Pearce said, 'He's a product of our academy and I've always been one who says you've got to have strong links with your academy at your club. For a young academy player to come and score the winning goal in a derby match is fantastic for him. He epitomised the spirit in the second half. He was shoulder to shoulder with anyone in terms of ability and endeavour.'

Of course, Forest and Derby share a closely intertwined history, largely revolving around Brian Clough, a fact Pearce is aware of more than most. As he grasped the Brian Clough Trophy, pride beamed across his face. 'The fact of who it's named after means a great deal to everybody in these parts, not just for me and Nottingham Forest but for Derby County as well. If anything, hopefully Brian, if he was watching from upstairs, he'd be proud of the performance by both teams today,' he said.

In a rather sad coda, Forest went on to lose their next two games, one of which was at Fulham when the Reds found themselves 3-0 down within 35 minutes owing to a Ross McCormack hat-trick, resulting in Pearce's sacking by the club he proudly represented as a player.

For Osborn, he continued to impress each and every new Forest manager that came in and out of the revolving door since Pearce, constantly scuttling about, covering every single blade of grass in a very Steve Hodge fashion, seeking the ball, receiving the ball and passing the ball in a way that would make Brian tell the other Forest midfielders, 'Give the ball to Benjamin, he can play football.'

We'll always have Ben Osborn's goal at Derby.

Chris Cohen vs Ipswich Town (2017)

CHRIS Cohen didn't score many goals for Nottingham Forest but when he did, they went all the way in to the back of the net and stayed there, just as they are burrowed deeply into the psyche of the fans that saw them.

Since signing from Yeovil Town in the summer of 2007, Cohen has pretty much seen it all. As if acutely aware of the severe emotional trauma he and his Yeovil team inflicted upon a whole generation of Forest fans on that May evening when Forest stared directly at a first Wembley play-off final, only to allow it to slip through their buttery fingers, Cohen has spent his time at Forest stretching every sinew and fibre of his body to ease the pain of that evening.

Although utterly synonymous with Forest for the bulk of his career, it wasn't always thus. Cohen learned his trade at the West Ham academy and earned attention when he became the youngest player to make the first team for 80 years at the age of 16 years and 284 days, a record since undercut by Domingos Quina and Reece Oxford.

It was December 2003 when Cohen got the nod from manager Alan Pardew to replace Matthew Etherington on 77 minutes and take his place alongside Jermain Defoe, David James and notorious red-card botherer, Thomas Repka. He had come a long way in a short time from playing for the superbly named Grays Cosmos in Norfolk as a kid to carrying out ball-boy duties at Upton Park a mere four months before his record-breaking debut.

First-team opportunities dried up at West Ham as they climbed back to the Premier League so Cohen made his way to Yeovil Town, initially for a month's loan, then for an extended loan and finally as a permanent signing. It was in his second season with the Glovers that Cohen and Arron Davies impressed so much that Forest made a £1.2m bid for their services.

Despite the initial excitement at such a capture residing especially with Davies after his brutal takedown in the second leg of the play-off semi-final at the City Ground in which he was nigh-on unplayable, it was Cohen who enjoyed a long and fruitful career at Forest. He notched his first goal on New Year's Day of 2008 with an equaliser against Huddersfield Town before Lewis McGugan snatched all three points with a startling last-minute winner for the ten men after Kelvin Wilson was sent off in the first half.

Initially deployed as a winger – sometimes an orthodox left-winger but just as often, on the right with a strong tendency to cut in – he gravitated towards the middle of the park as he grew more experienced and even deputised confidently and competently at left-back.

On a scouting report for *The Guardian* in January 2008, Steve Claridge noted, 'He is not a complicated footballer in his play – only in his positioning – he did his job defensively when needed and was prepared to help out his full-back, particularly when overloaded.'

While it is precisely this intelligence on the pitch that earned the respect of the Forest fans, the injuries he endured earned their sympathy.

He suffered his first serious knee injury against Derby County in September 2011 as he challenged for the ball yet twisted his leg in doing so. It seemed innocuous yet he lay prone on the turf as play went on around him, culminating in Derby's Jamie Ward sliding the ball home under Lee Camp for an equaliser from an improbable angle.

It was a painful day in many ways: Forest lost to ten men as Jeff Hendrick sealed the points with a clean strike from the edge of the penalty area. In terms of bad days at the office, file this one under 'very very dark'.

It took a year to recover but this Cohen did before amassing 57 appearances and once again cementing his place in the first team. Then it happened again against Burnley in November 2013. Typical of his commitment to the cause, he tried to play on and even succeeded in making a successful pass before sensing that something was seriously wrong. Indeed it was – a ruptured cruciate.

Once again, Cohen recovered and fought his way back before, once again, it happened. Again. Once again the opponents were Derby at the City Ground and once again it was September – this time in 2014. Britt Assombalonga found the net for Forest in a 1-1 draw under Stuart Pearce's reign but Cohen's career briefly hung in the balance. 'In the changing rooms after I said to the physio about ten times, "That's got to be it, I can't just keep doing it,"' he told *The Guardian*, 'And then I got in the car, and the first thing I think I did was ring my mum and just said, "I know what I've got to do."'

His recovery was already under way. But this time, not only did his knee require rebuilding, he would also have to recalibrate his playing style. No longer would he dive wholeheartedly into challenges. No longer would he put further stress on his knees by stopping suddenly. No longer would he put stress on the same part of his leg when accelerating. Something had to change so he got busy changing it.

He said, 'I can play the way that I used to. I just have to adapt the way I move and the mechanics of my movement. It's hard, but I think I can do it. I have been unlucky but you've got to be proactive. You can't just feel sorry for yourself and go, "You know what, hopefully I won't get unlucky again," which I have done after the first two. The physios were warning me [during the previous recoveries], and I knew what they were telling me was right but I was kind of thinking, "It'll be all right, I feel great."'

If there is a glimmer of good to come from such a story of misfortune on the pitch, Cohen found it. 'The best thing about being injured was that we got to share those early months with Frankie a lot more than if I'd been playing football,' he told *The Football League Paper*. 'I didn't realise how much hard work it is looking after a baby. I was able to give my wife a chance to rest and for me to spend time with my son.'

But there is more to Chris Cohen than a litany of injuries and bad luck; he was a provider of 'moments'. When Cohen smiled his big beaming boyish smile after scoring a goal, Forest fans all smiled with him – extra long and hard.

After his first cruciate injury, he returned to the fold and under the short-lived reign of Alex McLeish he opened the scoring against Derby at Pride Park, achieving some degree of closure after suffering the injury against the very same opponents. When Billy Sharp powered down the right wing and dug out a cross, the ball looped up into the air for Cohen to smash from the edge of the box. Instead, he fluffed his lines and struck the air yet implausibly, the ball bounced again, this time even more invitingly for him to slot home. This he did.

It mattered little that Ward equalised in the second half compared to Forest having Cohen back. He beamed an extra-wide grin as he wheeled away in celebration.

After his third injury, Cohen opened the scoring on the final day of the 2015/16 season against MK Dons, helping to seal a rare away win. He made his return earlier in the season on a dank day at Charlton Athletic in January to rapturous applause but when he stooped at the far post to chalk up his first goal of the season on the final day, that beaming smile made it all worthwhile.

Just for good measure, he chucked in a weird goal celebration in which he jumped clumsily into the air, banged himself on the head with his fist then crumpled to the floor. For an implausible third time, Forest fans had Cohen back and he was very welcome.

Exactly a year later, Cohen repeated the trick of scoring on the final day of the season and this time, it meant something deeper. After a bizarre campaign under Frenchman Philippe Montanier in which the Fawaz Al-Hasawi era finally lumbered to an inglorious end, Forest went into the game needing to win against Ipswich Town at the City Ground. Anything less and League One beckoned.

With so much riding on the game, it was little surprise to see the home team looking so jittery and it took a special save from Jordan Smith to keep them in the contest. When Britt Assombalonga smashed home a penalty just before half-time, nerves were eased, although not eradicated. More was required.

⚽ ⚽ ⚽

On 69 minutes, David Vaughan receives the ball and immediately the crowd urges him to 'shoooooot' from distance. He thinks better of it and lays the ball to his left to Cohen who has found a pocket of space. Still 30 yards out, he takes a touch to bring the ball under control, nudging it a few yards ahead of him, close to the Trent End goal. Again, 'shoooooot' reverberates around the stadium.

Cohen throws out his arms, swings back his left leg and blasts it. In a split second, the ball hits the top corner. In a split second, the tension is eased. In a split second, Forest are all but safe from relegation.

He's only gone and done it again – scored on the final day of the season and produced one of those very special 'Chris Cohen' moments that ranks alongside that goal against Blackpool at Bloomfield Road in the play-off semi-final, that goal against West Bromwich Albion at The Hawthorns which rounded off a sweeping move from back to front and naturally, alongside those redemptive goals against Derby and MK Dons.

He's not quite done yet though. Among the pandemonium, he hurtles towards the bench and jumps into the arms of a huddle of outstretched arms, including the physio team.

⚽ ⚽ ⚽

'Two of our physios were at my wedding,' says Cohen. 'I think they'd have made it to the top table if I'd been getting married this year because I've spent so much time with them.'

This moment though – blasting Forest away from peril and into life under new ownership after three career-threatening injuries – is more redemptive than the moment Andy Dufresne stands arms aloft in a Christ-like pose after crawling through 'five hundred yards of shit-smelling foulness' towards the end of *The Shawshank Redemption*. Catharsis never felt so good.

Bibliography

General:
Bickerton, B., *The Essential History of Nottingham Forest* (Headline, 2002)

Ian Storey-Moore vs Everton (1967)
Wright, S., 'Give it to Moore, he will score', *Bandy and Shinty*, Issue Two, December 2016

Peter Shilton vs Coventry City (1978)
Taylor, P., *With Clough, by Taylor* (London: Sidgwick and Jackson, 1980)

Frank Clark vs Ipswich Town (1978)
Clough, B., *Clough: The Autobiography* (Corgi Books, 1994)
Juggins, P., 'Alan and Liam', *Bandy and Shinty*, Issue Five, August 2017
'Frank Clark interview', *When Saturday Comes* website (September 1999)
Marples, D., 'In Conversation with...Paul McGregor' *InTheTopOne* website (February 2015)
Clough, B., *Cloughie: Walking on Water* (London: Headline, 2002)
Crossley, M., *Big Norm: Looking After No.1,* (Mark Crossley. Printed by Hickling & Squires, 2011)
Taylor, D. & Owen, J., *I Believe in Miracles* (London: Headline, 2015)
Butcher, T., *My Autobiography* (Highdown, 2005)

Colin Barrett vs Liverpool (1978)
Marples, D., 'In Conversation with...Colin Barrett', *InTheTopOne* website (April 2015)

John McGovern vs AEK Athens (1978)

Francis, T., *Clough: A Biography* (Stanley Paul, 1987)

Taylor, D., *Deep Into The Forest* (The Derby Books Publishing Company, 2009)

Marples, D., 'In Conversation with...John McGovern', *InTheTopOne* website (February 2015)

Ian Bowyer vs FC Köln (1979)

Taylor, D. & Owen, J., *I Believe in Miracles* (London: Headline, 2015)

Marples, D., 'In Conversation with...John McGovern', *InTheTopOne* website (February 2016)

Trevor Francis vs Malmö FF (1979)

Taylor, P., *With Clough, by Taylor* (London: Sidgwick and Jackson, 1980)

Francis, T., *My Forest Story*, NFFCTube (June 2016)

Wilson, J., *Nobody Ever Says Thank You. Brian Clough: The Biography* (London: Orion, 2011)

John Robertson vs Hamburger SV (1980)

Marples, D, 'In Conversation with...Jonny Owen', *InTheTopOne* website (September 2015)

'John Robertson Interview: Whatever Happened to JR?', *Sunday Herald* website (October 2012)

Pearce, S., *Psycho. Stuart Pearce: The Autobiography* (London: Headline, 2000)

Collymore, S., *Stan: Tackling My Demons* (London: CollinsWillow, 2004)

Taylor, D., 'Brian Clough and the Miracle of Nottingham Forest', *The Guardian* (October, 2015)

Steve Hodge vs RSC Anderlecht (1984)

Hodge, S., *My Forest Story*, NFFCTube website (June 2016)

Hodge, S., *The Man With Maradona's Shirt* (London: Orion, 2010)

Taylor, D., 'Bribed in Brussels: How Nottingham Forest fell victim to fixing scandal' *The Guardian* website (December 2013)

John Metgod vs Manchester United (1984)

Murray, S., 'The Joy of Six: goal celebrations', *The Guardian* website (December 2007)

Nigel Clough vs Manchester United (1986)

Clough, B., *Clough: The Autobiography* (Corgi Books, 1994)

McGrath, P., *Back from the Brink* (London: Arrow Books, 2006)

Clough, N., *My Forest Story*, NFFCTube, website (June 2016)

Hamilton, D., *Provided You Don't Kiss Me* (London: Fourth Estate, 2007)

Brian Rice vs Arsenal (1988)

Hamilton, D., *Provided You Don't Kiss Me* (London: Fourth Estate, 2007)

Marples, D., 'Number One is Brian Rice', *Bandy and Shinty,* Issue Three (March 2017)

Garry Parker vs Everton (1989)

Czech Forest, 'Nottingham Forest will always be an important part of my life, says Brian Laws', Czech Forest website

Berry, G., 'New Celtic Coach Garry Parker reveals how wife saved his life after stroke', *Daily Record* website (June 2010)

Neil Webb vs Luton Town (1989)

Juggins, P., 'Alan and Liam', *Bandy and Shinty,* Issue Five (August 2017)

Clough, B., *Clough: The Autobiography* (Corgi Books, 1994)

Pearce, S., *Psycho. Stuart Pearce: The Autobiography* (London: Headline, 2000)

Webb, N., *Wembley Again! Nottingham Forest 1985-1992* (Burton Joyce: Pineapple Books, 2008)

Taylor, D., *Deep Into The Forest* (The Derby Books Publishing Company, 2009)

Gary Crosby vs Manchester City (1989)

Crossley, M., *Big Norm: Looking After No.1,* Mark Crossley (Printed by Hickling & Squires, 2011)

Scot Gemmill vs Arsenal (1991)

McDonald, H., 'Scot Gemmill's picture paints a thousand words but his story begins with just two: the journey', *Herald Scotland* website (June 2015)

Clough, B., *Clough: The Autobiography* (Corgi Books, 1994)

Marples, D., 'In Conversation with…Paul McGregor', InTheTopOne website (February 2015)

Roy Keane vs Tottenham Hotspur (1992)

Juggins, P., 'Alan and Liam', *Bandy and Shinty,* Issue Five (August 2017)

Keane, R., *Keane: The Autobiography* (London: Penguin, 2002)

Clough, B., *Clough: The Autobiography* (Corgi Books, 1994)

Stan Collymore vs Peterborough United (1994)

Collymore, S. (2004), *Stan: Tackling My Demons,* London: CollinsWillow

Paul McGregor vs Olympique Lyonnais (1995)

Marples, D., 'In Conversation with…Paul McGregor', *InTheTopOne* website (February 2015)

Ian Woan vs Tottenham Hotspur (1996)

Woan, I., *My Forest Story,* NFFCTube website (June 2016)

Steve Chettle vs Bayern Munich (1996)

Blackburn, P., 'Chettle', *Bandy and Shinty,* Issue Four (May 2017)

Chris Bart-Williams vs Reading (1998)

Greenstreet, R., 'The Questionnaire: Chris Bart-Williams', *The Guardian* website (March 2001)

Andy Reid vs Sheffield United (2000)

Mackey, L., 'The Many Sides of Andy Reid', *Irish Examiner* website (January 2011)

Oliver, S., 'Andy Reid', LeftLion website (March 2013)

Hockett, S., 'Nottingham Forest? Didn't they win the European Cup twice?' *Bandy and Shinty,* Issue Two, (December 2016)

Julian Bennett vs Yeovil Town (2008)

Burnton, S., 'Bennett bemoans Forest's bad luck as crunch time approaches for Calderwood', *The Guardian* website (December 2008)

Dexter Blackstock vs Bristol City (2009)

Whittingham, C., 'The Four Year Plan – Review', Loft For Words website (November 2011)

Wes Morgan vs Notts County (2011)

Clifton, H., 'Nottingham: less looting but five police stations were attacked', *The Guardian* website (December 2011)

Ben Osborn vs Derby County (2015)

Clapson, S., 'Why ever-present midfielder Ben Osborn is so important to Nottingham Forest', *Nottingham Evening Post* (November 2017)

Taylor, D., *Deep Into The Forest* (The Derby Books Publishing Company, 2009)

Chris Cohen vs Ipswich Town (2017)

Claridge, S., 'Chris Cohen, Nottm Forest', *The Guardian* website (January, 2008)

Miller, N., 'Nottingham Forest's Chris Cohen relearns how to play after third cruciate injury', *The Guardian* (December 2015)

Ellis, A., 'Big Interview: Nottingham Forest captain Chris Cohen', *The Football League Paper* (December 2015)